PURSUING YOUR LIFE DREAM

Uncover the Destiny
Hidden in Your Heart

by Eastman Curtis

Harrison House
Tulsa, Oklahoma

08 07 06 05   10 9 8 7 6 5 4 3 2 1

Pursuing Your Life Dream:
Uncover the Destiny Hidden in Your Heart
ISBN 1-57794-685-5
(Previously published as *You Can Make It Happen*
ISBN 1-57794-419-4)
Copyright © 2002 by Eastman Curtis
P.O. Box 470290
Tulsa, Oklahoma 74147

Published by Harrison House, Inc.
P.O. Box 35035
Tulsa, Oklahoma 74153

Contents

Chapter 1

God Has Big Dreams for You!

And who knows but that you have come to the kingdom for such a time as this.

ESTHER 4:14 AMP

Do you know that God gave you something very specific to do in your life? You're not here just to survive as best you can. God has something more for you than that. Whether you realize it or not, God has a destiny for you, something only you can do. I'm not talking about doing the most "sensible" thing or doing what you think others expect you to do. I am talking about doing what God put in your heart to do—your life dream.

Maybe you don't know what your life dream is. Maybe you never thought about it. When God created you, He put a certain desire in your heart that would not only bring you joy and fulfillment in life, but would also accomplish His purposes for you. It's there in your heart. You may have to hunt for it, but it's there. Until you do something with that desire, you'll never know complete fulfillment.

I believe there are going to be a lot of people who, when they get to heaven, realize, "Hey, I could've enjoyed my life while on earth." The truth is, God wants you to enjoy your life here on earth. The life you were created to live should be a life of joy; living for Christ should not be a burden!

Whatever God has called you to do, it's going to be something you like to do. Some people think that in order to obey God, they've got to do things they really hate. That's not how God works. He works with our personality. After all, He's the One who gave it to us. Know that God has good things in store for you.

One of the greatest travesties in the world today is the teaching that everybody evolved from an amoeba into a monkey and then into a human being. When people buy into this lie, it totally destroys their sense of destiny and uniqueness. You didn't come from a monkey, and you didn't just happen along by chance. You didn't evolve from an amoeba or some cells that just happened to come together eventually to shape you into a human being. No. God formed you with a particular purpose in mind. He placed you here on the earth with a plan in mind for you. It is no accident that you were born. You were "fearfully and wonderfully made" (Ps. 139:14), and God put you here for such a time as this.

If you look in the book of Esther, you'll find an example of how God put the right person in the right place at the right time. There was a Jewish woman by the name of Esther who ended up in the Gentile king's palace. God gave her such favor with the king that he chose her to be his queen.

A man named Haman was scheming to destroy the Jewish people. At this time, no one knew that Esther was a Jew, not even the king. One day, Esther's Uncle Mordecai sent word to her about what was happening. He reminded her that God had placed her in this position for a very important purpose: to deliver the Jewish people out of the hand of Haman. "For if you remain completely silent at this time," he told her, "relief and deliverance will arise for the Jews from another place, but you and your father's house will perish. Yet who knows whether you have come to the kingdom for such a time as this?" (Est. 4:14).

God had raised Esther up and placed her in that specific position for that specific time and purpose. Esther did not know beforehand how she would be used in this position. She was chosen by the king because she was very beautiful and because she had his favor.

We may not always understand why God wants us to be where we are. It may not even seem like it's a great place. It is so important to do exactly what God tells you, and not to think the job is insignificant. Who knows but that you have come into the kingdom of God for such a time as this!

Called Before You Were Born

Before you were even a thought in your parents' heads, God had a plan for you. Look at what Paul the apostle says in the book of Galatians: "It pleased God, who separated me from my mother's womb and called me through His grace" (Gal. 1:15). Paul says that he was called while he was still in his mother's womb.

Now look at Jeremiah 1:4-5. "Then the word of the Lord came to me, saying: 'Before I formed you in the womb I knew you; Before you were born I sanctified you; I ordained you a prophet to the nations.'" God planned for Jeremiah to be a prophet even before he was born.

You may be thinking, *Well, that's great for Paul and Jeremiah. But I'm just little ol' me.* God is no respecter of persons. Just as God called Paul, Jeremiah, Elijah, Isaiah, and all the great men and women of God you hear of, He has also put a call on your life. Before you took your first breath, God had already placed His hand upon you.

> "My frame was not hidden from You, when I was made in secret, and skillfully wrought in the lowest parts of the earth. Your eyes saw my substance, being yet unformed. And in Your book they all were written, the days fashioned for me, when as yet there were none of them."
>
> PSALM 139:15,16

Paul tells us in Romans 8:28-30 that God predestined us and called us according to His purpose. And in Ephesians 1:11 we are reminded that we are "predestined according to the purpose of Him who works all things according to the counsel of His will."

In 1 Corinthians 2:9, we are told that God has prepared incredible things for those who love Him. When we take time to find out what that plan is, we'll discover that His plans are big. God has huge dreams for each of us.

You may be saying to yourself, *Well, I've been going in this direction for a long time. It's too late for me to change.* Or maybe you're saying, *Well, Eastman Curtis, God gave me a dream when I was a little kid.* I knew it was from God, but too much time has gone by, too much has happened in my life, and now I'm 40 years old, and it feels like my time has already passed.

Well, I've got a good word for you. God says in Joel 2:25 that He'll restore to you the years that the cankerworm, the caterpillar, and the palmer worm took from you. He'll restore all those years you weren't heading toward your dream, all those years you were going the wrong way. God will give you back all the time the devil has stolen from you, all the time spent dealing with setbacks and roadblocks and doing a bunch of stuff He never called you to do. It's never too late. Don't just sit there looking at the sunset, moaning, "Oh, look at my life. Look at the time I've wasted." Stop it!

Look at the sunrise. Look and see the destiny God has for you. Choose to see what God has in store for you and determine that no circumstance, no person, no devil, nothing is going to keep you from your dream. Grab hold of His vision for your life. You need to see it and do something about it. As long as you have breath left in you, it's never too late.

Moses was 80 years old when he began heading in the direction God had for him. God had actually called him and shown him what He wanted him to do when he was still a young man. For 40 years he hid out in the wilderness, herding sheep. It wasn't until he was 80 years old that he set out to lead 3.5 million people out of the captivity of Egypt into the Promised Land. Three point five million people! And he did it on foot at 80 years old!

And then there was Caleb. He was 85 years old when he walked up to Joshua and said, "Josh, I'm just as able to take the mountain that God promised me when I was forty years old as I am now. It's not too late for me. That's my mountain. I can do it." (Josh. 14:6-12.) And Caleb got his mountain.

Colonel Sanders was 65 years old when he started building his Kentucky Fried Chicken enterprise. He was still living off $105 a month from Social Security! And Ray Kroc started the first McDonald's when he was 52 years young. And he was 66 when he finally saw his dream of having 1,000 McDonald's around the U.S. come true! Ben Franklin signed the Declaration of Independence at 70 years old, and John Wesley was still preaching all around the nation on horseback at the age of 88! There are some who journey out onto the mission field when they are 60 or 70 years old.

So don't tell me it's too late for you. Don't you believe it! God has a plan for you. That plan may have been sitting dormant in you for years, but that's not because God didn't put it there. It's never too late to change directions and grab hold of God's best for you.

Imagine you are climbing up a ladder and, when you get to the top, you realize, *Hey, I'm climbing up the wrong building. I'm supposed to be over there.* So, what do you do? Do you just plop down and stay there anyway? No. You climb back down, grab hold of your ladder, and move it over to where it's supposed to be, then get back on that ladder and climb up the right building! When you find out you've been heading in the wrong direction to fulfill your dream, don't stop; pick yourself up and run in the right direction.

Now, not everyone can change directions at the same pace. For some people, it's like turning a little motor boat around. All they need to do is turn the wheel and zip it around to head in the right direction. When you are sailing in a big ocean liner, it's another story. You can't whip it around like a small boat. It takes a little more time to turn that ship around. You have to start turning the wheel, and eventually you will be headed in the right direction.

For example, if you're single and you don't have any baggage such as large debts and a family—you can just turn the wheel of your life and zip in the right direction. But if you've got a family and a home and responsibilities, it will take more time and effort to change gears. You will have your wife or husband, children, mortgage, and car payments to consider.

It may be that the destiny God has for you will not mean a big move. You may be positioned in the right place, and with a few small adjustments you can be on the right track. Your destiny does not require you to leave town or change jobs. In fact, God needs people in all kinds of places, jobs, and situations. Often people go to a university or Bible college with unique gifts and callings, but when they graduate, they come out a clone or copy of someone else. That's not God's will. You are an individual.

Just Be You

I remember one of the greatest revelations I ever had when I first stepped into ministry. I was walking on a golf course, thinking about my heroes of faith: Smith Wigglesworth, the apostle Paul, Terry Law, R.W. Shambach, Brother Copeland, Brother Oral Roberts, Kathryn Kuhlman. Faith people I admire. Rather than being encouraged, I got really discouraged, thinking, *I could never be like them. I could never preach like Shambach. I could not do that.* I began to compare myself to other people, which is something we should never do.

As I did, I began to feel so inferior and inadequate. Suddenly the Spirit of God rose up on the inside of me and said, *I don't need another apostle Paul. I've had one. I don't need another Smith Wigglesworth. I've had one. I don't need another Terry Law. I have a Terry Law. I need an Eastman Curtis.*

And that's exactly what God says about you. He has raised you up for such a time as this. God has a destiny for your life. He wants you to fulfill the purpose for which He has called you. Don't think you have to run off to the mission field or Bible school to fulfill your dream. That might be the case, but not necessarily. What fits you? There is a perfect match for your personality and desires.

Some people think that if they're going to please and obey God, they've got to give up everything they like, get a dugout canoe, run off to preach to people wearing designer fig leaves in the Amazon, and eat fish eyes until they finally die of malaria. If God has called you to preach to natives in the Amazon, you're going to love it! It's going to be a passion that burns inside you, something that gives you a thrill like nothing else.

I've seen people who are truly called to be missionaries. They love what they're doing. When they come back to the States for a visit, they say, "This is great, but I've gotta get back to the Congo. My heart's back there. I've gotta get back." They even like the food there. They like the adventure and the wildness of it. That's because God put that passion in them. They are doing what they were created to do.

Don't try to be someone you are not. Be who God made you to be and do what He's called you to do. If He's called you to be an insurance salesman, praise God! Be the best insurance salesman you can be. Do it with all your heart. God needs insurance salesmen to advance the kingdom of God. Or maybe He's called you to be a doctor or a businessman or a truck driver or a waitress. God needs people in all walks of life.

If everyone were a preacher or a missionary overseas, where would we be? We would be in trouble. God needs you to take your place in His plan. He doesn't need you to take someone else's place.

It is really frustrating when I ask people what kind of work they do and they just sort of hang their head and say, "Well, you know, I'm just a homemaker." Don't you dare belittle the call of God to be a homemaker! It's one of the greatest calls of God there is! The Bible says in the book of Malachi that God desires godly offspring. (Mal. 2:15.) One of the things most precious to Him are your children. When God calls you to be a homemaker, you can hold your head up high. And when someone asks you what you do, throw your shoulders back and unashamedly say, "Glory to God! I'm a homemaker. I'm training up my kids in the way they should go. I'm pouring into them. I'm depositing into them." Do not be ashamed.

Belittling the call of God on your life is like slapping God in the face and telling Him He didn't pick the right thing for you to do. God knows what He's doing. Whatever dream He has given you to fulfill in life is just as important as what He has given anyone. Everyone has a place in God's kingdom in order to make it happen. In Romans 11:13, Paul is talking about his ministry—and calling—and says, "I magnify my ministry." Paul was an educated Jew preaching to the Gentiles. Jewish people did not associate with the Gentiles. Paul was not ashamed of what God had called him to do. He didn't hang his head and make excuses for his ministry.

Paul persecuted the Christians before he became one himself. His shame for his past could have kept him from his calling, but instead he rose up, held his head high, and magnified his ministry. That doesn't mean he was arrogant. That's not what this Scripture is saying. Paul knew he needed God to accomplish his call. He was declaring that he wasn't ashamed of the ministry God gave him. Paul chose to walk out his destiny with all his might, and nothing could stop him.

You may come across some people who will try to convince you that your calling isn't important. God says it's important, and that's what matters. Sometimes you may find people speaking from the pulpit who make you feel guilty or inferior if you're not an apostle, prophet, evangelist, pastor, or teacher. You might be tempted to think, *Well, I'm just second best in the kingdom of God.* No, you're not! Don't you believe that! God needs Holy-Spirit-filled electricians, plumbers, beauticians, and used car salesmen!

Every part of the body is vital. Even toenails count. If you've ever lost a toenail, you know what I'm talking about. Man, your whole body gets into a twist if you rip a toenail off. Do not blush about what God has given you to do. He needs you to give it everything you've got and stand tall.

God will perform miracles and wonders to bring about your destiny. There won't be room for arrogance. Because, trust me, it is going to take miracles! Be confident in what God has given you to do. It's hard to move forward in the things of God if your head's hanging down low. "Therefore strengthen the hands which hang down, and the feeble knees, and make straight paths for your feet" (Heb. 12:12). "Be strong in the Lord and in the power of His might...and having done all...stand" (Eph. 6:10,13).

I remember when there were scandals in the ministry. You could pick up a copy of *USA Today*, and every day on page two you could find out the latest. As I traveled on airplanes, people would ask, "What kind of work do you do?"

I sure didn't feel like magnifying my ministry then. I'd just hang my head and say, "Well, I'm a preacher."

They'd look at me and say, "You're a what?"

"I'm a...ah...blumbbbbbbb. I'm a traveling minister."

I hoped they wouldn't associate me with those scandals, because I was ashamed of the ministry. The Spirit of God told me, *Don't you blush. Don't be ashamed. Don't hesitate. You stand strong in the gifts and the calling that I've given you. Be confident in what I've given you, and you're going to see increase come as you magnify your ministry.*

Don't be ashamed. God wants you to magnify your calling just as Paul did. It all starts with knowing your dream. You need to know what God has called you to do.

God Wants You Fulfilled

When you begin to turn in the direction God has for you, you'll not only see Him restore all the time lost, as He promises in Joel 2:25, but you'll experience the greatest fulfillment you've ever known. Nothing compares with being in the will of God and doing what He has designed for your life.

Look further in Joel.

> I will restore to you the years that the swarming locust has eaten…. You shall eat in plenty and be satisfied, and praise the name of the Lord your God, who has dealt wondrously with you.
>
> JOEL 2:25,26

God wants you to be satisfied. There are many people who can't find any satisfaction in life because they've never found their true destiny. As you do what God has given you to do, "you shall eat in plenty and be satisfied." He wants you to be fulfilled. He wants you to achieve your destiny—even if you do get a late start. He will help you cross the finish line, as long as you're willing to cooperate with His plan.

In verse 26, He says He has "dealt wondrously with you." God has exciting things for you. You can expect great things to take place in your life when you step into your destiny.

God has a great destiny for you, but He needs you to make it a reality. God did not create us to be robots or puppets. He made us with partnership in mind. Not only do you need Him to fulfill what He has called you to do, but He also needs you to do it. He's depending on you. He won't force you to walk out your destiny. It's a choice you have to make.

At thirteen years old, I was a mother's worst nightmare. I did a lot of dumb stuff. My mom and dad loved me with everything in them, and, because they loved me, they wanted me to do the right things. No matter what they did to influence my decisions—no matter how many times they lectured me, no matter how many times they grounded, disciplined, or tried to convince me to do things differently—the ball was still in my court.

My mom would have long talks with me. She and Dad would try to encourage me and steer me in the right direction—even whoop me into making right choices—but I'd still flat out make the wrong decisions. They wanted what was best for me, but they kept watching me settle for second best—and sometimes way less than second best! After all was said and done, the choice was still mine. I was seventeen years old when the lights finally came on and I realized that Jesus Christ loved me and had something better for me.

It was then that I made a decision to stop living with second or third or fourth best and receive God's best for me. I asked Christ to come into my heart, and He delivered me out of darkness and into His kingdom of light. I realized that I needed to make some changes if I really wanted God's best for me.

In Deuteronomy 30:19, the Lord even tells us what the best choice is: "I have set before you life and death, blessing and cursing; therefore choose life!" Before I was born again I chose death and the curse. Even after I was saved there were times when I made the wrong choices, but God had something better in mind for me just like He has for you.

In verse 20, He tells us why we should choose life: "that you may dwell in the land." The land is the place where His promises are fulfilled. I am not talking about a physical land but a spiritual land. This land is where the blessings are. It's where fulfillment lies. It's where your destiny is.

God has big dreams for you. God can't make you choose the best that He has for you. He allows you to decide. He wants you to choose life and blessing. He wants you to choose the dream He has for you. But He won't twist your arm to make you do it. He wants you to use your free will to choose what He has for you and to move into your destiny.

It's important to understand that God is the One who gave you your dream. It was not your Aunt Sally or your pastor or anyone else who thinks they know what you should do with your life. Look at what Paul says in Galatians.

> For do I now persuade men, or God? Or do I seek to please men? for if I still pleased men, I would not be a bondservant of Christ. But I make known to you, brethren, that the gospel which was preached by me is not according to man. For I neither received it from man, nor was I taught it, but it came through the revelation of Jesus Christ.
>
> GALATIANS 1:10-12

Paul wasn't called by men, but by God. He goes on to say, "I did not immediately confer with flesh and blood" (Gal. 1:16). In other words, he's saying, "When I got this revelation from God, I didn't immediately blab to everyone about it. I thought about it. I dreamed about it. And then I began to pursue, not what people thought I should do, but I began to pursue what God Almighty told me to pursue." And that's what God is telling us today. Find and choose God's destiny for your life.

Chapter 2

Discovering Your Life Dream

People are searching to find their place in the world. That's because God put that desire in each person. It's because He has given each of us a specific destiny to fulfill, and, until we discover it and move in it, we're not fulfilled. Many times this very desire to find fulfillment leads people to experiment with all kinds of things—things like drugs, sex, cults, and all kinds of activities that only end up leaving them emptier than before. Why? Because these things are fakes to God's true purpose for their lives. They don't really fill the void. Their true destiny is still sitting there inside them, waiting for fulfillment.

People often think destiny and destination are one and the same, but they are not. Destiny is a journey, not an arrival place. It's a journey that takes you to your destination. Destiny is the process of accomplishing the dream or desire God puts in your heart. It's something you press into and pursue. When you head in the direction God has for you and move into your destiny, you're fulfilling the purposes of God for your life.

Some of you may be thinking, *Boy, if I just knew what God wants me to do with my life. If I just had a crystal clear picture of what He's called me to do, I'd give myself 100 percent to it. Man, I'd focus on it. But how do I know what God wants me to do with my life? How do I figure out what my destiny is?*

First, you don't have to strain your brain to come up with a dream. You don't have to invent something to do with your life, because God has already given you a dream. You just need to discover it—then step into it!

You may still be scratching your head and saying, "Yeah, right. But how do I discover it?" Discovering your dream can be one of the most difficult but most rewarding things you will ever do in your life. Discovering your dream is the beginning of a more fulfilling life—the kind of life God designed for you.

Seven Things That Help You Discover Your Destiny

It would be nice if Jesus appeared to each of us and handed us a telegram that says, "Here's what I want you to do." Most of the time God doesn't tell us our destiny that way. I have discovered seven things that will help you discover God's will for your life.

1. Determine What Your Desire Is

The first way is found in the book of Psalms. "Delight yourself also in the Lord, and He shall give you the desires of your heart" (Ps. 37:4).

As you can see from this Scripture, our part is to delight in the Lord. Our responsibility as humans is to make God the greatest delight of our lives. That means we delight in Him more than anyone or anything else—more than money, people, our vocation, or things. When we do our part, God does His. His part is to give us the desires of our heart. As He sees us delighting in Him, He responds by giving us the desires of our heart. Now, that doesn't mean He's only going to give you the desire for ministry. He knows you have other desires too. You want a nice house, nice car, beautiful spouse, and wonderful family. Is there anything wrong with these desires? No. God wants you to succeed and have many good things in life. "This Book of the Law shall not depart from your mouth, but you shall meditate in it day and night, that you may observe to do according to all that is written in it. For then you will make your way prosperous, and then you will have good success" (Josh. 1:8). And in Proverbs 3:6, we're told that God will direct us and crown our efforts with success when we put God first in everything we do.

God wants you to succeed. He's the One who told us to "seek first the kingdom of God and His righteousness, and all these things shall be added unto you" (Matt. 6:33). What does He mean when He says "all these things"? If you look at the rest of the chapter in Matthew 6, you know that He's talking about clothing, food, and all the things we like to have in life.

There's nothing in the Bible that says it's wrong to want things. Wouldn't you want your kids to have nice things that would truly make them happy? So why wouldn't our heavenly Father want the best for us too?

But we must have our priorities right. Think of it this way. Even though you love your kids and want to see them blessed, what would you do if you could see that they were just plain greedy and selfish and were always demanding more and more from you without ever a thank you or a hug or anything that shows their appreciation for you? And what if the things they went after were just destroying them? Would you want to keep giving them these things—things that were more harmful than good?

When your kids are loving on you and wrapping their arms around your neck and telling you how wonderful you are, don't you want to find ways to bless them even more than they've ever dreamed?

God loves to bless us. As long as what we desire is not immoral or illegal, and as long as it's not in contradiction to God's Word and conforms to His will for our lives, we have a right to believe God for that thing.

Now, there's something else that happens when we delight in the Lord. Our desires begin to change. The closer we get to God and the more we walk with Him, the more we begin to desire what He desires for us. Something begins to happen inside us, and soon we desire things we never even thought about before.

After I was born again, I still played drums at a country bar. I was saved, excited about Jesus, and going to heaven, and I would get up and witness to people between shifts. I would sit down with my Bible and tell others about the Lord, and they would give their heart to the Lord right there in the bar. Sometimes I would lead more people to the Lord in bars than I would in churches. Some churches were harder to preach in than the bars!

I played and ministered in the bars at night and really liked the money, but the closer I got to God and the more He became the delight of my life, the more I found that I didn't like going to those country bars. I didn't like the smell of cigarette smoke and the stench of beer poured all over my drum set. My desires began to change.

Things began to happen in my life, and I knew it was time to move on. God was doing something new in my heart. I wanted to spend more time in church, Bible studies, and prayer meetings instead of the bars. I loved reading and studying the Word of God, and I noticed that I became more passionate toward certain things. I delighted in the Lord, and He gave me the desires of my heart.

Manipulation from other people has caused many Christians to think that in order to serve God, they need to become a preacher or a missionary. Not so! God is the One who places His desires in your life, so don't let someone else slap their desires on you. I can't tell you how many people I have talked to who have felt condemnation for not going into the ministry.

They think they do not really love God if they do not go into the mission field or pastoral ministry. But, as I said in Chapter One, if that's where God has really called you, then He'll put those desires in your heart and you'll love it. But God doesn't expect you to trudge through life doing something you really can't stand, or something you don't even have a natural ability to do.

It's important for you to recognize that the desires in your heart—a heart that delights in the Lord—are not bad. Some people think that all desires are fleshly, carnal, and cannot be from God. They think that if it sounds like something fun to do, it surely can't be spiritual—as if you have to groan through life doing things you hate just to please God! I don't know who came up with that idea, but it definitely wasn't God.

The Word of God is full of Scriptures that make it clear that God wants us to enjoy our life—and that includes the destiny He's given us to fulfill. It also means it's okay to enjoy the things God gives us. First Timothy 6:17 tells us to trust "in the living God, who gives us richly all things to enjoy." Did you notice that it says that we're to "enjoy" the things God gives us? And in Joshua 1:15, the people of God are told to "enjoy" the land God gave them. Enjoying life is God's idea.

If all the desires of your heart were bad, why would God say in His Word that if you delight in Him, He intends to give them to you? (Ps. 37:4.) Would that make sense? No. God does not contradict Himself. Listen to what Jesus tells us in Mark 11:24 KJV. "Therefore I say unto you, What things soever ye desire, when ye pray, believe that ye receive them, and ye shall have them." Doesn't that sound like He knew we'd desire some things?

The truth is that God puts desires in us so that we'll do what He designed us to do. The desires are there to act on, not to resist. I am not talking about carnal desires here. I do not want you saying, "Well, Eastman Curtis said it was okay to go and live with another man's wife because I sure do desire her!" I'm not talking about those kinds of sinful desires! Those are the desires of the flesh, and we must resist them. When you really love God and follow Him with everything in you, God says, *You want that? I want to give you that. I love you so much, I just want to bless you with that.* As long as it's not illegal or immoral and it's in the Word of

God and conforms to His will for your life, you have a right to believe God for that thing.

Godly desires will rise up in you when your heart is right toward God and you delight in Him with all your heart. It is important to understand that the "godly desire" in you might not sound all that "godly" when you first consider it. It could be that you have a desire to work on old cars. Or maybe you have a desire to own a restaurant or a business or to work with children. Just because the desire does not sound spiritual does not mean God did not put it there. As I said before, God needs people in all kinds of places to do all kinds of different things for Him.

What's pulling at the inside of you? What is it you most want? You may be saying, "Yeah, right. Like I even know what I want to do!" If you're not sure what desires are in your heart, start by asking yourself what you really like to do most. What's most important to you? What would you like to achieve if you could? It may not be completely clear at first, but if you'll begin to prayerfully search your heart, God will show you.

Get a piece of paper and start writing your thoughts down. Putting your desires on paper helps to clarify them, to make them real to you. Even if you end up with a huge array of things, that is okay. Ask God to give you a closer look. Do all these things tend to go in one general direction? (e.g., Do they revolve around leading people to Jesus Christ? working with computers? teens? kids? Do they tend to involve traveling or talking to people?) Most of us have lots of different interests, but there's usually just one thing that God has put in our heart to really go after.

When you find out what that one thing is and begin to walk in it, then you will be able to focus your time, attention, and gifting on that one thing.

Now, that doesn't mean that you cannot be multi-tasked, nor does it mean that one thing won't involve many different things to get you there. If, for instance, you are called to be a pastor, that does not mean you just jump right into the pulpit and start preaching. There are many things you need to learn before you are prepared to pastor a church. You need to learn some people skills, for instance. How do you do that? You might start by working with people. You might get involved in the youth ministry, the children's ministry, or the helps ministry. You might usher, greet people, or change diapers in the nursery. You become involved in various aspects of church ministry, and all the while, your heart's yearning to pastor a church.

There can be a lot of seemingly different things going on in your life during the preparation time. And you might not even know right away what your true calling is. That's okay. Just keep moving in the direction your heart (your spirit) is pulling you. If you're drawn to work with small children for a while, do it.

If the desire in your heart keeps you there, that may be your true calling. Sometimes that's a place you need to be for a short time to get to your higher calling. Do not become upset if you start out in the nursery, because, after a year or two, you may feel led to move out into other areas such as the mission field or teaching teenagers. God has a plan for you, and sometimes that plan has some stepping stones that move you from Phase A to Phase B to Phase C to Phase Destiny!

So, move in the direction God is drawing you. Start with some of the things He has already put in your heart to do. The more you walk these things out, the more refined your vision will become.

2. Determine What Your Passion Is

> Then His disciples remembered that it was written, "Zeal for Your house has eaten Me up."
>
> JOHN 2:17

When Jesus saw what was going on in the temple, He was stirred up. When He saw how the moneychangers were cheating the people, the zeal for His house consumed Him.

It rose up in Him and moved Him to action. He didn't calmly walk into the temple and mildly say, "Well, okay guys. Now you know this isn't right." No sir! Clark Kent turned into Superman! He walked in, grabbed a rope, made a whip, and swoosh! He got down to business with that whip, knocked over tables, drove out the moneychangers, and cleaned house. His zeal was ripping!

That'll mess up someone's theology. God is a good God. He wants people heading in the right direction. Relationships are important to Him, but He hates religion with a passion. When things were keeping people from a relationship with God, it fired Him up. The zeal for His house consumed Him.

So, Jesus had zeal—a passion—for His Father's house. What do you have a passion for? What gets you all fired up? When God puts a vision in you, you will become passionate about certain things—things that have to do with that vision, that dream in you.

When you talk to some people, all they want to do is talk about children's church. "We've just gotta do this for children's church. Children's church is where it's at, man!" It is because that's their passion. That's what God has called them to.

Then some want to talk about the Internet. "Man, if we'd just get on the Internet, we'd never have to buy another TV spot again! Everyone's on the Internet. We will reach the world with the Internet. All we have to do is hit the Internet." Well, that's their passion.

So, what's your passion? That's another way to find out the will of God for you. You can tell where your passion is by what really riles you up. One time I was watching television and eating a bowl of cottage cheese with pears in it. It was not my favorite, but I was eating it. My wife, Angel, was on some weird diet thing, so I was doing it with her. It is amazing the things you'll do for your wife or husband because you love them.

An evangelist comes on TBN and starts talking about his ministry to children, how essential it is, and how great it is. And I'm like, "Yeah, man! Amen! Come on, Bud! Go!" I love this guy. He's been a big influence in my life and I'm having a great time. But suddenly he makes this statement: "We really need to focus on the children, because you know as well as I know that the teenagers of this generation are just too far gone."

When he said that, I felt like making a whip. I got mad, threw my spoon at the TV, cottage cheese and all! *Splat!* "No way!" I said. "This generation is not too far gone!"

I don't care what anyone else says. I believe that this is the generation that's going to win us the greatest revival in the history of humanity! I get passionate about that! I get excited because it is my passion to reach this generation for Christ.

So, how do you know what God has called you to do? Number one: What are your desires? Number two: What is your passion? What really pushes your button? What is that thing that really lights your fire? When you discover that, you're on your way to finding out God's will for your life.

3. What are your gifts and talents?

The third way you can discover God's will for you has to do with how He has gifted and talented you.

The book of Romans tells us that "the gifts and the calling of God are irrevocable" (Rom. 11:29). Notice that "the gifts" is plural, and "the calling" is singular. The King James Version says "without repentance," which literally means "irrevocable." That means that God won't give them to you, then take them back, and give them to you again. God is not like that.

When God puts a dream in your heart, He doesn't take it back. They're not a loan. The more you use them, the more refined they will be and the better they'll become. The more you exercise them, the more developed they're going to be. The less you use them, the less developed they'll be. But you can't use up those gifts.

When it comes to a gift or talent, some people think, *Well, I'm just saving it. I'm holding it.* No. You need to use it. Take that gift and begin to utilize what God has already given you.

Sometimes people are gifted in certain areas and, because it's so natural to them, they don't even realize it. The gift is something that naturally flows out of them without their thinking of it. Encouragement from others can help them recognize their abilities as gifts from God. When they do their thing, people may say, "Wow! Look at that! That's incredible."

And they say, "Oh, really? I just threw it together."

"Wow. Man, I wish I could do something like that."

"Aw, anyone can do that. It's easy."

"No, I can't do that. That's a gift you've got. It's a gift."

And that may be the first time they ever thought of their ability as a gift. That's why the ministry of encouragement and exhortation is so important in the body of Christ. If you see someone doing something well, tell him or her! Be a Barnabas. (Or, for you women, be a "Barnabette.") Be an encourager. When someone has treated your kids well in the nursery, or if a schoolteacher has really blessed your children, encourage them in the work they do. When you see something that you like about someone, don't keep it a secret. Tell them. You might even discover that your gift and calling is to be an encourager.

With the gifts God gives each of us, there is a calling behind them. He wants us to develop those gifts because we are likely to need them to fulfill our callings. Encouragement can help to develop those gifts. I know I want to be an encourager. Tell people around you, "You've got gifts and a calling." They need to hear it. So what if they don't know what they are yet. Sometimes people have to go on a treasure hunt, but the gifts are there. Praise God!

4. What works?

Sometimes people are beating their head against the wall, trying to fit into the wrong mold. Some say, "Well, I feel God has called me into full-time ministry." But they assume that, in order to prove their love for God and fulfill their calling, they have to be a pastor, missionary, evangelist, or teacher. They love God, but they get all confused about how to show that love. So they substitute their love of God for the service of God, and that can pull them off course.

If God has truly called you to be a pastor or a missionary or an evangelist, then go after it. But remember, not everyone is called in these areas. Some may be called to make a lot of money for the kingdom of God. Maybe you need to make that million-dollar sale so that you can take the commission and sow it into the kingdom of God. There's nothing wrong with that. It's wonderful, in fact. That's needed in the family of God. It takes money to accomplish God's will. So that's just as much a calling as the one who's going overseas to minister the Word of God. Now, I don't mean that you should make money itself your total focus. If you're called to bring money into the kingdom of God, you'll have a passion to bless the kingdom. That will be the driving force: to support the works of God versus making money to look good or to please yourself.

Ask yourself, "What works?" I know a man who planted a church. He started out with twenty-five people, and now twenty years later, he's worked himself down to fifteen people. After twenty years of that, I think it is time to realize, "Hey, maybe I've dropped my ladder on the wrong building." Pay attention to what works.

I like what John Osteen always said, "Follow the blessings." Find where the blessings are for you and head in that direction. Follow the blessings.

Following the blessings does not mean giving up without a fight. Sometimes you just need to keep pressing on toward your dream even when it's a battle. Just because you have some hurdles to get past or some delays does not mean you should immediately throw in the towel. There are times when you must fight for your dream, because the devil might not be so eager to let you get it too easily. Learn to recognize the difference between fighting for your true vision and banging your head against the wrong wall.

Sometimes you have to open your eyes and notice a few things. If, for instance, you've been going in a certain direction to pursue your dream for a long time—I'm not just talking about a month or two; I'm talking about years—and it just isn't happening, it may be time to ask yourself if it's really from God. It may be time to get on your face before God and say, "Lord, is this really what You have called me to do? Or am I just spinning my wheels?"

As I said, there are times when it can take a while to get there. Many things can get in the way. It doesn't necessarily mean it's not from God. (I'll talk about that in another chapter.) But if it just doesn't seem to be working and there's no peace in it, it's time to reevaluate, because when God calls you to do something, it works.

The Bible says, "Let your light so shine before men, that they see your good works and glorify your Father in heaven" (Matt. 5:16). When people see the good works—the successful works—you're doing, it blesses people and it glorifies God. So, go after the blessings. See what's working and follow that.

5. What bears witness in your spirit?

God will show you just as much what not to do as He'll show you what to do. There will be times when you'll start heading in a direction and feel like this is the way to go. You pray about it and the desire is there, but when you start to walk through that open door, you realize something is not right. Something in your spirit stops you.

Danger signs are going off. Your husband or wife freaks out. You realize you might not be in the will of God, or it could be that it's God's will but the wrong time. Timing matters.

So, what do you do when the red lights are going off? You just take a step back and find where the peace is. Then you follow the peace—like the yellow brick road. Follow the peace. Follow the peace. Follow the peace. What's that? That's the witness of the Holy Spirit in your spirit.

Let me give you an example. When we finished working with the ministry here in Broken Arrow some time ago, I thought, *Bless God! We're going back down to Florida.* I kept thinking about going to Florida because it seemed like the natural thing to do. That's where we founded our ministry. That's where we had started. But every time I'd start to take a step to Florida— *honk!* I'd get a check in my spirit. *No, don't do it! Stop. Don't go in that direction.* And I just couldn't go that way, because I didn't have peace about it. I have missed God before and the peace left. I did not want to do that again. Every time we tried to head back to Florida, we'd get a strong sense that, no, there's something different.

So we stayed in Broken Arrow. The longer we stayed, the more I started to love this place. The more I delighted in the Lord, the more I loved it here. And now I just love Tulsa! I love Broken Arrow! This is a Florida boy talking, so you know this is a God thing! And now, when we go to Florida, I can't wait to get back to Tulsa. Everyone says, "Uh, Tulsa?" And we say, "Yeah, it's great. They don't have all the crime there. We know and love people there, and we pray for each other when trouble comes. They love God. Ministries are growing everywhere. Man, I love Broken Arrow! I love Tulsa." That's what happens when God puts desires in your heart.

So, follow the peace. Don't get out of peace. Stay where the peace is. Now, sometimes there will be an excitement—like an anxious excitement—but, when you're doing what God has called you to do, you still have the peace down inside. You might get a little anxious about doing something you have never done before, but if you want what you have never had, you have to do what you have never done. You begin to stretch, your faith is exercised, and you think, *Well, I've never stepped out this far before.* But still, you have the peace. So you keep going, and soon you begin to see the blessings flow.

6. *Godly counsel*

What does your godly counsel say? Notice that I used the term "godly counsel." Not just any counsel, but godly counsel. What does your godly counsel say? Not all the counsel that comes from the pulpit is godly. It is your responsibility to test what you hear against the Word of God. Some people have hidden agendas and control issues that affect their counsel. Choose to listen to godly counsel. There are those who love God and really do want the best for you.

A while back a couple came to me and said, "Eastman, we're feeling an unction to go to the Dallas/Ft. Worth area. We believe that God's going to do some great things and explode some business opportunities for us down there. We just started coming to Destiny Church, and we love Destiny, but...."

These people were gifted. I could see it flowing out of them. Their potential was so obvious, and I had them slotted within our church. I knew exactly what I wanted them to do, and now they're telling me this. The more they talked about the potential opportunities in Dallas, the more excited they became. They told me they'd prayed the thing through and it was something they felt they needed to do.

I just looked at them and said, "You need to do what's in your heart."

If I had been looking out for what was in my best interest, I would have said, "No. Don't go. You'll be cursed if you leave this place. The enemy is going to pound you. Your finances will dry up. You're going to get in a car wreck. You'll get sick." I could have steered them away from where they were really supposed to be. That is manipulation, and God is not like that.

Consider your godly counsel. What do your friends say—the friends who really know the Lord? I do not mean the ones who just know about God, but the ones who know God and follow Him with all their hearts. What do they say?

Proverbs 11:14 tells us, "Where there is no counsel, the people fall; but in the multitude of [godly] counselors there is safety." I inserted "godly" in front of counselors there because that's the implication. The Bible mentions a number of situations where people (e.g., King Saul and other kings) sought some very ungodly counsel and got into trouble.

You have to be careful with whom you share your dream. One time I began to share my dream of putting a commercial on MTV with a certain pastor. It was the biggest mistake I ever made in my life. When I told him what I wanted to do, he got this lofty look on his face. "Why do you want to give God's money to secular TV?" he said. "I mean, MTV! That's perverse. Why do you want to give God's good money to the devil?"

"I'm not giving it to the devil," I told him. "I want to get a commercial out there where the sinners are."

He just folded his arms, looked at me, and said, "Eastman Curtis, you can't raise that much money. That's impossible for you to do." He kept on telling me I couldn't do this and I couldn't do that. And pretty soon, I was whipped. I felt all beat up. I started to think, *Oh God, I can't do this. I've got this dream, but I can't do it.* I read in my Bible where it says, "I can do all things through Christ who strengthens me" (Phil. 4:13). So I thought, *I need to find an encourager. I need to find someone who at least believes in me a little bit.*

I have a good pastor friend who is a visionary, and we get together and pray. He is a dreamer. He's the kind of man who looks beyond his little kingdom and sees the whole kingdom of God. So I went to him—well, really, I ran to him—and told him what was in my heart. And I asked him what he thought.

He loaded his finger, stuck it in my face, and said, "Eastman Curtis, you're going to miss God if you don't do it. God has given you this vision. God gave you this gift. If anyone can do it, you're the man God has called to do it."

What was that? That was godly counsel. Godly counsel puts something in you instead of taking something out of you. Godly counsel seeks what's good for the kingdom of God, not just what's best for someone personally or what is his personal opinion.

I'm not saying you should run all over trying to find someone to just agree with you. That's not what I'm talking about. It's not about asking someone to agree with your vision. It's about seeking out and listening to those who have the heart of God, those who are willing to encourage you to do the will of God—even if it costs them a personal sacrifice. That is godly counsel.

7. *To what can you give your all?*

What is that one thing you can pour yourself into? What excites you and thrills your soul to the point where you can dive into that thing headfirst? Very few people ever do that. Very few people ever give themselves fully to anything. Yet the Bible commands us to do this. Paul told Timothy to do this very thing in 1 Timothy 4:14-15: "Do not neglect the gift that is in you, which was given to you by prophecy with the laying on of the hands of the eldership. Meditate on these things; give yourself entirely to them, that your progress may be evident to all." Notice that he said, "Give yourself entirely" to the gift God has given you.

What would happen if everyone in the body of Christ gave themselves entirely to the gift that God has placed in their life? I don't think the world would ever be the same.

So, in summary, if you want to discover your God-given dream, ask yourself:

1. What one desire is burning in my heart?

2. What's my greatest passion?

3. Where are my God-given gifts, talents, and abilities?

4. What works?

5. What bears witness in my spirit?

6. What does my godly counsel say?

7. To what can I give my all?

Then, as you begin to move in this direction, trust the Lord to confirm your calling. If your heart is right toward God and you really desire to do His perfect will, you do not have to worry that these things will pull you off course. If for some reason you start to move in the wrong direction, God is well able to let you know. He did it for the apostle Paul. He will do it for you. And remember, it is a lot easier to turn a vessel that's moving than one that's just sitting there.

Chapter 3

Dare To Do Something New

Do not remember the former things, nor consider the things of old. Behold, I will do a new thing.

ISAIAH 43:18,19

God wants to do something so incredible—something so awesome—that it can't even compare to what has been done in the past. He wants to blast through everything of old and "do a new thing." He even tells us when it's going to happen. "For I am about to do a brand-new thing. See, I have already begun! Do you not see it? I will make a pathway through the wilderness for my people to come home. I will create rivers for them in the desert!" (Isa. 43:19 NLT). Now is the time for God to do a new thing.

God is a now God. He is not the I was God. He's not the I'm going to be God. He's the great I AM. (Ex. 3:14; John 8:58.)

God wants us to be open to Him to do a new thing in our lives today.

Have you grown complacent, stagnant, and apathetic? If so, it's time to embrace God's new thing for your life, time to push aside the old things that are keeping you back and step into something new. It's time for your promotion, time for advancement. It's time for you to look up and see the big destiny God has for you.

God is faithful and true. He wants to take us to a higher place in Him. He wants to take us into our destiny and make our dreams a reality. He wants to move us from all that is old and stale and give us something new.

But if we're going to receive God's new thing, we've got to let loose of the old things. God tells us, "Do not remember the former things, nor consider the things of old" (Isa. 43:18). It's hard to grab hold of something new if you're still hanging on to the old. God has something better so turn loose of the old and grab hold of the new.

A lot of people get stuck in a rut, and they don't want to accept change. "Well," they argue, "this is the way we've always done it. This is the way it's been done in the past. This is the way Mom did it. This is the way Grandma did it. So this is the way it's got to be."

There is a story I heard years ago about a woman who would always cut the ends off of every roast she made. Her daughter grew up and did the same thing with her family's roasts. Then the granddaughter grew up and did the very same thing. One day the husband of this third-generation daughter asked his wife, "Why do you cut the ends off that roast? I love that part!"

"Oh, I have to do that!" she told him.

"Why?"

"Because Mom always did that."

"Well, why did she do that?"

"I don't know. I'll ask her."

So she asked her mom, and her mom said, "I don't know. I've just always done it that way. It's how my mom always did it."

"Well, why did she do it?"

"I don't know. I'll ask her."

So she asked her mother and discovered her mother always cut the ends off the roast like that because she had only one pan, and the roast would only fit in it if she cut the ends off.

All that time, the two generations after her thought they had to do it that way too because that's how their mothers had done it.

Sometimes we hang on to a certain way of doing things for the sake of tradition. We cling to old habits and traditions that don't really mean anything. They are not biblically based, and sometimes they do not even make a lot of sense. But we hang on to them because "that's the way we've always done it." We refuse to do anything differently because "we've never done it that way before."

Look at what Isaiah 43:18 says in the New Living Translation: "But forget all that. It is nothing compared to what I am going to do." Sometimes we can get so focused on our past that it keeps us from going forward. If we want something that we've never had, we must step into some areas that we've never stepped into before. So go ahead and begin to do things you've only dreamed of doing.

Dare To Do Something Different

George Eastman

Have you ever heard of George Eastman? He was born in 1854.[1] As an adult, he worked as a bookkeeper for a bank in Rochester, New York, and he had a hobby—something that he really enjoyed doing. In his spare time, he loved taking photographs using his big, box-like camera. He would have to hold up the flash powder, climb under that covered camera, and say, "Now look at the birdie!" And *boom!* There was a huge explosion of powder from the flash going off, and it would burn the image of the photo inside on a piece of glass.

George Eastman was so enthralled with photography that he thought everyone would love taking pictures if they could. But it was such a cumbersome process with those big old cameras that most people didn't want to mess with it. So George Eastman determined to make a camera that anyone could use.

When people heard of his idea, they said to him, "You can't do it. It's never been done before." Eastman, aware of the need for a simple procedure for taking pictures, introduced something in 1889 which was called 'flexible film' and a simple box camera that he called the Kodak. The new film and camera, backed by an aggressive advertising plan, made Kodak a household name. More than 100,000 of his cameras were sold the first two years, an unprecedented achievement in the photographic industry.

Over 100,000 sold! This was back in 1889. Isn't that incredible? Everyone told him it couldn't be done, but he did it because he had a dream.

The story goes on to say that by the turn of the century, Eastman had employed over 3,000 people throughout the world. Not only was he a pioneer in photography, he founded a medical school, a technology center, and music schools.

He did things that had never been done before. He pioneered the exportation of U.S. goods to foreign markets. He would go into foreign markets and sell his cameras. He was also a pioneer in establishing health services for his employees and retirement plans. No one had ever had a health plan for their employees. On top of that, he offered profit-sharing plans to his employees. He took care of his people.

What about all those who said it couldn't be done? They were like a lot of people who have more faith in the way things have always been than in the way things can be. They wanted to keep things the same and would rather throw cold water on new ideas than encourage someone to be a visionary.

T. L. Osborn

The great missionary evangelist T. L. Osborn received a certain revelation regarding healing years ago when he was in Jamaica. Up to that time, people were individually laying hands on the sick in healing crusades. He would give a call for people who wanted to be healed, and literally hundreds of people would come forward.

One time while he was in Jamaica, he saw a huge crowd and realized that there was no way he could pray for them all individually. He felt so much compassion for them and wanted to minister to each one, but he didn't know how it could be done. How could he lay hands on hundreds of people? He began to pace back and forth because he was really torn up about it.

The Spirit of God reminded him of Mark 16:17-18: "These signs shall follow those who believe: In My Name they will cast out demons, they will speak in new tongues... they will lay hands on the sick, and they will recover." These signs will follow them that believe. You've given an altar call for salvation. These are now believers who need healing. The Holy Spirit was reminding him that these were believers looking for healing. The Spirit of God instructed him to have them lay their own hands on whatever part of their body where they needed a healing miracle.

Now, understand that this was in the 1940s, and this was not being done. People had been prayed for individually, with the laying on of hands, and that is the way it had always been done. Because this was something new, T.L. Osborn didn't have people lay hands on themselves as God instructed him. He wanted to make sure he had really heard from God, so he went through the Scriptures and couldn't find anything contradicting it. Three crusades later, he had the people lay hands on themselves and pray for their healing.

If you were to watch the footage of some of his meetings, you would see mighty miracles take place before your eyes. You would witness huge goiters hanging off of people's necks. The cameras showed people laying their own hands on the enlargements of their thyroid glands, and you'd see the goiters literally shrink and shrivel up. People laid their hands on their legs and lept out of wheelchairs or jerked their leg braces off. Blind eyes were opened and cataracts melted out of eyes. But most of those people would have never had the opportunity to be ministered to this way. They might never have received their healing if T. L. Osborn hadn't begun to do something that had never been done before.

Billy Graham

I remember hearing Billy Graham tell stories of how people thought he was nuts because he brought in contemporary gospel music at his crusades. He'd minister to teenagers and use contemporary music to reach them. It was revolutionary. People never thought of doing anything like that in ministry back then. Many people thought he was going secular, that he was way outside the box. Billy Graham saw hundreds of thousands of teenagers brought into the kingdom of God through his crusades. What might have happened if Billy Graham had listened to all the criticism and pulled out the contemporary music? Who knows how many came to his crusades because he was playing music they liked. We have to be willing to be radical to accomplish God's dream.

Hunger for More

I remember when my wife, Angel, and I first started ministering. I'd go to churches and see maybe five or ten people born again. I still get excited when I see that happen, but I was a full-time evangelist, and my heart was to see people come into the kingdom of God. That's what I have done since I was seventeen years old, and that's what was burning in my heart. As exciting as it was to see these become born again, I longed to reach more people, to bring more into the kingdom of God. I remember praying, "God, there's got to be more. I know You want to do more. Show me what

I can do. Show me how I can be more effective, how I can see more results with what I've got. What can I do, Lord, to bring more people in?"

God began to show me some different things I could do through altar calls and some ways I could improve our ministry. I received an invitation from a man to speak at his business conference. He was a wonderful Christian businessman. He said to me, "Eastman, what I want you to do is preach for fifteen minutes, just like at your church. Give it everything you've got. Then, at the end, I want you to invite people to receive Jesus."

That's the kind of person I like, one who wants an altar call with a bunch of businessmen, most of whom have probably never even been in a church all their lives. So I stood up there, shared my testimony, preached for only fifteen minutes, and gave an altar call. We saw over five thousand people respond to receive Christ in that one altar call.

I could have been satisfied with just five or ten people at a time as before, but I wanted more. If I want to step into realms I've never stepped into before, I have to be willing to do what I've never done before.

If I had listened to the people who told me not to get on television, we wouldn't be seeing the wonderful miracles we're now seeing. As a result of the altar calls we give on our television show, thousands of people have called in to ask Jesus to be Lord of their lives!

If you want what you've never had, you've got to do what you've never done before. We must turn loose of the old and boldly advance into the new things God has for us.

I talked to a man who had trained fighter pilots in Vietnam. He said most of the fighter pilots whose planes were shot down had an opportunity to bail out. They could have just pushed the eject button and escaped by parachute, but most of the pilots would not push that button because they liked to stay in the familiarity of the cockpit.

In other words, they liked the cockpit of a crashing plane more than the unfamiliarity of the parachute. They chose to go down with the airplane instead of taking a chance with what was not familiar to them. They did not know what would happen if they pushed the eject button, so they would not do it. And it cost them their lives.

Many people have done that same thing spiritually because they were too afraid to step out of their comfort zone and into the plan of God. God has a plan for each one of us. He urges us to step out, to dream big, and to do what we've never done before in order to have what we've never had before. *Step out into deeper water,* He's saying. *Come on. I have things planned for you that, if I told you now, you would not believe it. It's bigger than you know. It's huge. If you're going to have it, you've got to step out. You've got to push that button, walk that walk, pray that prayer and seize the moment. No one can do it for you. You've got to take hold of your dream and run with it.*

Sometimes Christians think, *Well, if God has something for me, He'll get it to me when He wants.* So they just sit there waiting for God to accomplish the plan for them. But God needs us to carry the plan out. He needs us to fulfill the vision He gave us. He needs us to make our dream come true. Now, I don't mean that God won't help us accomplish our dream. Of course He will. Why do you think He calls the Holy Spirit our Helper? God wants to partner with us in His plan. He created each of us for a purpose and with a dream to fulfill, but He won't force us to do anything. He won't fulfill our dream for us. That's why He gave it to us.

Many times we're afraid to push that button in the cockpit because we're not familiar with it. We're afraid to take the chance because we're secure where we are. Thank God for where we are and thank God for what He has brought us through. But it's time for us to move on to bigger and better things. I want to keep advancing. I want to keep pressing in to get all that God has for me.

Growing Up

In praise and worship and in our intimacy with God, there can be areas where we become very comfortable. I remember the first time I went to a charismatic church. It felt a little weird when the pastor said, "Just lift your hands and worship God." When I finally dared to lift my hands for the first time, I only raised my hands a little from the elbows. I couldn't stick my hands straight up. It was a new thing to me, but after a while I got used to it. Now it's natural and easy.

I also remember the first time I began to speak in other tongues. It was such a head rush to me, but as I became familiar with it, I found myself doing it often. I'd do it driving down the road in my car. You can have camp meeting in your car. Thank God for cruise control, because when I feel the anointing flowing through me, my driving speed increases!

We always need to be stretching and growing and moving into some new areas in God. If you've never lifted your hands as an act of surrender to worship God, I encourage you to do what you've never done before. The Bible tells us that we're to lift our hands without wrath or doubting. (1 Tim. 2:8.) David said in Psalm 63:4-5 NLT, "I will honor you as long as I live, lifting up my hands to you in prayer. You satisfy me more than the richest of foods. I will praise you with songs of joy." God's Word commands us to worship Him with everything we've got! (Deut. 13:3, 30:6; Josh. 22:5; Matt. 22:37; Luke 10:27.) God instructs us to do this. We don't speak in tongues just because it feels good.

God wants to bring us to a place we've never been before. If we want to step into God's new work, we are going to have to leave behind the old. Quit thinking, *Well, God did it this way before, so I guess that's the way He always wants to do it.* Stop limiting God. Let God get out of the box you're keeping Him in. Let God be God, and remain open to what God desires to do in your life.

A Good "Thang"

God's new thing is a good thing. Now, for those of us from Oklahoma, that would be "new thang." It is important that we understand what God's talking about in Isaiah 43:19. He doesn't say, "I'm doing a new method." And He doesn't say, "I'm giving you a new experience." What He does is wipes the slate clean and says He's doing something so wonderful that we can't compare it to anything else, because, if we could, we would limit ourselves.

In Proverbs 18:22, it says, "He who finds a wife, finds a good thing." Before I was married, I knew women. I had sisters and a mother. I love my momma. She is the one who brought me into this world, fed me, changed my diapers, and cooked meals for me. I love my sisters even though sometimes they would torment me—because that's a sister's job. But I knew they'd stand up for me.

But I can't compare my relationship with my momma or my sisters to the relationship I have with my wife. I'm telling you, it's a good thing! There's a special intimacy that you can enter into with a wife that you can't have with anyone else.

I remember the first time I kissed my wife. She wasn't my wife then, but I did ask her to marry me the next day. When I kissed her, she looked up at me and said, "Honey, don't kiss me like you kiss your sisters."

So then I told her what happened to me when I was eight years old. I was playing spin the bottle with some friends. Understand that I wasn't saved yet and my parents weren't Christians. The bottle that I spun landed on a certain girl and I was supposed to kiss her. I'd never kissed a woman in my life other than my sisters and my momma, so I pursed my lips and got ready for a kiss. I approached her lips with my eyes shut because that's how they did it on TV.

I wish I had never shut my eyes, because when my lips touched her mouth, I realized that her mouth was open to the size of a cavern. And, man, when I opened my eyes I thought I saw three cavities, two molars, and a root canal.

That freaked me out, so I started screaming and spitting. I ran into the bathroom and gargled with mouthwash. I brushed my teeth. I thought I was contaminated for the rest of my life! Remember, I was only eight years old, and I didn't even like girls that much then for that to happen—ugh! That really affected me. After that, whenever I would kiss anyone, I'd just keep my lips pursed real tight.

That's how I kissed my wife the first time. When I told her the story about that kiss, she just laughed and said, "That experience really affected you."

Well, when I dared to kiss her the right way, I thought, *Oooooh, baby, that's it!* I asked her to marry me that next day! (She can really kiss.)

I had to forget what had affected me in the past and move on to something much better. If I had never been willing to let go of that spin-the-bottle experience, I would have never gotten to the oooh-la-la! That's why the Word says we're to forget the former things. We need to get that old stuff out of our minds because there's a new dimension God is bringing us into. And, praise God! It is a good thang! "He who finds a wife finds a good thing" (Prov. 18:22).

I just gave you a physical example, but sometimes we do this spiritually. There are areas where we'll stop and refuse to go any further. Maybe it's because we've had a bad experience in our past. Maybe we saw something happen to Grandma or to someone else, so we just slam on the brakes. We need to understand and believe that God has some good things planned for us. He wants us to step into His goodness and grace. He wants us to move into areas we've never moved into before. But we can't do that until we turn loose of the old and grab hold of the new.

The Bible also talks about "things" in Mark 11:24. "Therefore I say to you, whatever things you ask when you pray, believe that you receive them, and you will have them." What is Jesus talking about here? What shall you have? Look at that word. Whatever things you ask for in prayer are what you will get. What are you asking for? Are you willing to ask for what you've never had before? Or are you going to settle for second best? Are you going to settle for asking for what you're comfortable with, or are you willing to go further?

Remember that you will get what you ask God for. If you can only ask Him for the things you've seen Him do for you in the past, that's all you're going to get.

Or will you dare to step in and start dreaming dreams you've never dreamed before? Are you ready to do some things you've never done before? When you start doing this, you're moving into God's dreams, because God has BIG dreams for you. His thoughts are higher than your thoughts, and His ways are higher than your ways. (Isa. 55:8,9.) Don't hold back. Don't forfeit the big things God has for you for the safe things of which you're familiar.

Stop Looking Back and Start Stretching Forward

> Jesus said to him, "No one, having put his hand to the plow, and looking back, is fit for the kingdom of God."
>
> LUKE 9:62

It's good to thank God for the good things He's done in our lives, but that's not where we need to stay. It's not where we need to focus. Rejoice in what God has done for you and through you, but realize that these things should not captivate you. They're not meant to hold you and keep you there, but to provoke you to move on for more. God's blessings are there to cause us to advance. Have you ever tried to keep moving forward while looking over your shoulder all the time? What does that do? It slows you down, doesn't it? It is hard to make good progress forward when you keep turning around to look at what is behind you.

If all your might and all your dreams are wrapped up in your past, you're not going to get to your future very quickly. If all you can do is talk about "the good old days," then that is probably as far as you will get. Go ahead and be thankful for your good old days, but don't stay there! It doesn't matter if you're 9 days old or 99 years old. God still has a great future in store for you. You're not too young or too old to move into your destiny.

We've got to keep moving ahead. We've got to keep advancing. Stop looking over your shoulder. Don't "set your hand to the plow" (Luke 9:62) and then say, "Man, I remember when it used to be like such-and-such. I remember it was so good back then." Look ahead! God has a great future for you. But if you're living in your past, you'll never obtain your future. That's why God tells us in Isaiah 43:18-19 that, if we want His new thing, we've got to forget the former things, "nor consider the things of old." We've got to turn loose of the old and grab hold of the new.

In Luke 5, Jesus saw three fishermen—Simon Peter, James, and John—cleaning their nets after a bad night of fishing. So He got into Simon's boat and asked him to pull out a little from the land so He could teach from the boat. After Jesus taught for a while, He turned to Simon and said, "Launch out into the deep and let down your nets for a catch" (Luke 5:4). But Simon was thinking about the past and how he and his fellow fishermen had labored and sweat all night trying to catch fish but got nothing. He's thinking, *Man, I just cleaned my nets, and now you want me to throw them back out—in daylight? Fish do not come up to the boat in the daytime.* So in verse 5 he said to Jesus, "Master, we have toiled all night and caught nothing...." Keep in mind, Simon's a fisherman by profession, and he knows that you normally have to fish at night to succeed. Trying to catch fish in the daytime is not something he has done before. So, Simon's thinking that what Jesus just told him to do doesn't make much sense on a practical level. But look at what he says in the rest of verse 5. "Nevertheless at Your word I will let down the net."

Are you ready to say "nevertheless" to Jesus when He asks you to launch out into the deep? Are you ready to say, "Well, I may not understand it, Lord. It doesn't make any sense to me. But, because You say so, I'll do it." Are you ready to launch out into places you've never been before? Are you ready to try something you haven't tried before?

Look at what happened when Simon did what Jesus told him. "And when they had done this, they caught a great number of fish, and their net was breaking. So they signaled to their partners in the other boat to come and help them. And they came and filled both the boats, so that they began to sink" (Luke 5:6,7). When Simon did what he'd never done before, when he dared to launch out into the deep, God gave him not only one boat full of fish, but two—and those two so full they were about to sink! He got himself a net-snapping, boat-sinking harvest!

What if Simon had said, "Well now, Jesus, I've already worked and worked, and it hasn't gotten me anywhere. I just don't see any reason to try anything different." He would have never seen the miracle of God, that's what. Sometimes we work and work and work, but it doesn't seem to get us any further along. It's time to do it God's way and realize that your old way of doing things isn't working. Launch out into the places God has for you, and do what you've never done before to have what you've never had before.

We need to be willing to do things differently sometimes. Occasionally I feel like just turning the order of the service all around at my church just to get us out of thinking in a rut. God doesn't want us in a rut. He wants us to move into the new thing He has. Sometimes we need to move over and let God be God, but so often we continue to be in His way and He is unable to take us further along.

> And when Peter had come down out of the boat, he walked on the water to go to Jesus.
>
> MATTHEW 14:29

Notice that only one disciple knew what it was to walk on water. Twelve of them had the opportunity, but only one stepped out of the boat when Jesus said, "Come." Only one responded to that word and began to do what looked like an impossibility. Granted, he began to sink when he started looking around at the circumstances, but Jesus was right there to catch Peter the minute he needed it. Only one of Jesus' twelve disciples will get to testify about this when he gets to heaven. "Hey, I was out there walking on the water with Jesus! That was so cool."

Every one of us has the opportunity to step out of our "boats" of familiarity into the exciting place God has for us. But, sadly, many never do. Too many would rather stay in their secure little boats where they will never experience all that God has for them in life. Don't get stuck in your boat and become satisfied with where you are. I hate that word "satisfied." Stay hungry for more and pursue the plan of God. Go after your dream. So what if people say it can't be done. It doesn't matter what people say. We've got a more sure word of prophecy. (2 Peter 1:19 KJV.) All things are possible to him who believes. (Mark 9:23.)

Are you ready to dream a dream and take a leap of faith? Are you ready to step into some areas you've never been in before and move into what God has for you? When you're willing to do this, you're going to see how, all of a sudden, miracles will start happening. You take a step and you are out there walking on the water with Jesus. Jesus is your Source. Keep your eyes on Jesus, and He will keep you moving forward in the things of God. It's how you will get to your God-given destiny.

Dare To Dream BIG

God has a big dream for you. He's got big plans for you—plans uniquely tailored for only you. He is eager to show you His dream for you; just dare to push the button, dare to reach out, grab hold, and dream BIG. He is waiting for you to step out of the boat and do what few people have ever done. It doesn't matter who you are in the natural. It doesn't matter if you've got a great education or no education at all. It doesn't matter if you're a man or a woman, black or white, American Indian, Hispanic, or Asian. It doesn't matter if you're young or old, smart or not so smart. God is raising up men and women from all walks of life and from every color, race, and background. It doesn't matter where you are or how you were brought up. It doesn't matter which side of the tracks you came from. God is looking for people who will step out of the boat, dare to dream the dream He puts in their heart, and get on with carrying it out for Him.

Henry Ford

Henry Ford was not a very educated man, nor was he known to be the systematic type, but he was what people called inspirational.[2] In other words, he would tend to obtain ideas through inspiration more than through facts. He was also an idealist. Thank God for idealists. And Henry Ford had a dream. He wanted to do what people said was completely impossible to do, to put a car in every person's driveway. He wanted every American to have a car of his own. That was his dream. But back in his day—at the turn of the century—cars were so expensive that there was no way to produce one that would be affordable to the average American. It couldn't be done.

Henry Ford thought outside the box and imagined ways to make what was impossible, possible. In 1913 he did something that had never been done before. He came up with the assembly line. Now, that may not sound like a big deal today, but back then it was something that hadn't been done before. The idea was to have a bunch of workers put cars together working as a team, with each worker doing only one thing over and over again. This way, each laborer would get good at one thing and the whole line would move efficiently as everyone did his or her part. People had never heard of anything like that.

After Ford developed the assembly line, he hired people to work the line and paid them five dollars a day. Back then that was good pay, so he didn't have a hard time getting laborers to work for him. All that each worker had to do was one thing. The car would come by, and they would screw the bolts on or tighten up some things; they would put the whole car together like that. That is how they were able to increase production and keep the cost of each car low.

Henry Ford was a dreamer. He had a dream in his heart and he saw it come to pass. And today it is not unusual to see two and sometimes three or more cars in someone's driveway because one man had a dream—a dream people said couldn't happen.

I don't know if Henry Ford was saved, but I do know he was an idealist. He had a vision. He had a dream. He didn't let other people limit him. He didn't let other people steal his dream. He didn't limit himself. Many times people limit the dream and the desire that God has for their life, and so many die without ever having fulfilled that dream.

When God begins to give us His vision and His dream for our lives, sometimes we can become intimidated and think, *Oh God! That's too big. I don't know if I can do that.* And, if we're not careful, our insecurity and sense of inferiority can knock us down so that we can't move forward into

God's purpose. If the dream in your heart doesn't seem big to you, then you are not dreaming big enough. If it's small enough for you to accomplish with your own gifts and talents and efforts, it's probably not even from God. When God puts something in your heart, it's so huge that, unless He intervenes, you'll utterly fail. God wants to be a co-laborer with us. He wants us to lean on Him and then watch Him do miracles for us. So, if the vision in your heart seems too big for you to accomplish, it probably is. That's when you need to get excited about it, because that's when you can know that God's going to step in to do some great and mighty things to help you carry it out.

When God began to share His plan with Moses, Moses reacted by saying, "No way, God! You can't mean me." But God told him He certainly did mean him. There was no mistake about it. "But God," Moses argued, "with all due respect, Lord, I—I—I think You've got—got—got the wrong man. I'm just not good with words. Listen to me, Lord. How—how—how am I supposed to lead all these people out of Egypt? What do You mean, talk to Pharaoh? I—I can't even talk right. I stutter when I talk." But the Lord knows His plan. "You're the one, Moses. You're My man for this job. You are the one I have chosen to deliver My people from slavery. You're the one who's going to bring them out, Moses. But don't worry. I'll be with you all the way."

Now, here's Moses, who was raised in the Pharaoh's palaces, the one who had the best of everything and all the palace training and all a leader needs to do the job. But Moses was about as insecure as they come. Look at Exodus and see for yourself. Moses did not want the job. Even after God assured him that He'd be right there to help him through the whole thing, Moses still tried to wriggle out of it. He wriggled and squirmed in his inferiority so much that he finally managed to irritate God. "Okay," God sighs. "Fine. I told you I'd help you and enable you, but that's obviously not enough for you. I'll get your brother, Aaron, to do the talking."

Moses accepted his destiny and moved into it and experienced miracles after that! He needed some BIG TIME miracles. And so will you when you move out into your destiny, because God has something for you that is beyond your own ability.

Don't be surprised if God puts a dream in your heart that's bigger than you are. It's good if it stretches you. We all need to have our faith stretched and worked more. That's how we grow. It's how we advance into our destiny. You cannot accomplish it in your own strength. You might get a taste of pavement—as in falling flat on your face. This is what happened to Moses.

Years before God spoke to Moses from the burning bush, He put a compassion for the children of Israel in the heart of Moses. He was preparing him for his destiny. Moses watched how the Egyptians persecuted the Hebrew slaves, and it really got to him. The Hebrews were actually his relatives. In Exodus 2, he was born Hebrew but had been adopted by Pharaoh's daughter and brought up in Pharaoh's palace.

When God plants His destiny in your heart, you start to feel a passion in that area. Moses had a real burden for the children of Israel, but that's not where he went wrong. It wasn't wrong for him to get upset when he saw the children of Israel being mistreated. It's not a bad thing to feel righteous indignation over injustice. God does, after all. God put His own burden and compassion for His people in the heart of Moses. The problem occurred when Moses tried to take matters into his own hands when he saw an Egyptian beating a Hebrew. He killed the Egyptian, and when he found out that the Hebrews knew what he did, he ran into the desert and hid for years, until God called him from the burning bush.

Moses tried to carry out his destiny in his own ability, and he got into trouble. Have you ever tried to do something of God in your own strength? It doesn't work. There have been times when I've tried to get up and preach "sugar sticks." That's what we preachers call messages that we have preached so many times that they're burned into our hearts. We can get up any time and preach them. We have them down pat. There have been times when I've gotten up to preach one of these sugar sticks, and it just falls flat and nothing happens. Sometimes I'll stutter and stammer through the whole thing and it doesn't come out right. That's called falling on your face, and it happens when you try to do something in your own ability. I'd much rather do things in God's power and ability.

Expand Your Vision

Once when I was invited to do an introduction at Oral Roberts University, Richard Roberts got up to speak. As he began speaking, he suddenly stopped, looked over at me, and said, "Eastman, that church you're building is too small. It's too small." Then he went right back to preaching his message.

I sat there thinking, *Okay, Lord. I'm stretching.*

Again, Richard Roberts stopped in the middle of his message. "Eastman," he said to me, "I'm telling you the church you're building—the Spirit of God is talking—the church is too small. That 2000 feet you're planning. It's too small. God is saying, I'm going to do something big there."

So my faith was stretching. The church is too small. As I walked out, Richard grabbed me and said, "Eastman, the Spirit of God told me."

"I know," I said. "The church is too small."

Then he said, "Yeah, yeah, yeah. But remember Psalm 37:23, 'The steps of a good man are ordered by the Lord.'"

We have to take steps to get to our dream, and the Lord orders our steps.

We found sixty-one acres just up the road from where we were planning the church and made a deposit on it. We're not going to get too comfortable to move on. We're going to keep growing and keep expanding the dream. And, as this church continues to grow and develop, we're not going to stop there. We're not going to get stagnant where we are. We're going to keep advancing. We're going to plant more churches and sow into people. We're going to keep blessing other ministries and sowing into them. We are going to change the world, but we have to keep dreaming. We can't get too comfortable, too satisfied, too apathetic. We've got to keep going forward, keep moving ahead into God's bigger vision.

Many times it's so easy to stop at the first revelation we get. Look at Martin Luther, for instance. He had a great revelation from God: the just shall live by faith. (Rom.1:17.) What a revelation! It was out of this revelation that the Lutheran church was birthed. Luther realized that people couldn't get to heaven by being good enough, but only through faith in Jesus Christ. Luther helped countless people realize that they could go directly to God because of what Jesus did and no longer had to go through the priest for forgiveness. They could now go to God the Father through Jesus Christ.

Many denominations were birthed out of the Azusa Street revival who received the revelation of praying in the Spirit and speaking in tongues with interpretation—which is wonderful—but they stopped there.

Henry Ford dared to dream big. He pursued his dream until it came true. In 1938, when he had the monopoly on the whole car thing, he suddenly stopped advancing. He had developed the Ford car and made it affordable for every average American. He had developed the amazing automobile industry. It was huge and it was skyrocketing. He decided he wasn't going to change. He would keep producing Model T's. Here was this amazing man who started something that had never been done, and ironically, he stopped progressing.

In the 1930s, General Motors surpassed Ford Motor Company and the Model T's died out. General Motors decided to embrace change.

So many times we hold on to our security at the expense of grabbing on to something new. We resist change and it slows us down. Even after you've accomplished some big things for God, don't stop there. Keep advancing. Keep progressing. Don't get stuck in that boat.

God is doing a new thing. He's looking for people who will move out of mediocrity, men and women who will step out of complacency and will hunger for whatever God has for them. I don't want to stop going forward in the things of God. I don't want to grow stagnant. I want to keep moving, keep building, and keep advancing.

Are you ready to take a step of faith and dare to make it happen?

Chapter 4

Steps to Fulfilling Your Life Dream

Then the Lord answered me and said: "Write the vision and make it plain on tablets, that he may run who reads it."

HABAKKUK 2:2

Once you know what your dream is and you're ready to launch out into the deep, where do you go from there? How do you actually fulfill your dream?

There are some practical things you can do which will set things into motion.

Write It Down

The first thing we have to do to step into our destiny is to write it down. Get out a piece of paper and write out what's in your heart to do. Write down the dream and the vision God has given you. Something happens when you do this. As you begin to write these things down, something takes place in the supernatural. It activates the power of God to solidify your dream. It helps you see the vision more clearly, take inventory of what you have, and evaluate it. I remember the first time I did this. My wife and I had talked about where we thought we were heading in our ministry, but nothing really began to happen until I wrote it down. And, when I wrote it down, something happened. It was definitely something supernatural.

Very few people will really take the time to write their vision down. They will make all kinds of excuses. "I'm too busy." "I'm too old." "I can't do that because of this or that." But, until you write it down, it's going to just sit there. You can talk all you want about it, but there's something powerful about writing it down.

I once took a time management course that stressed the importance of writing things down. This was such a revelation to me. I never realized that it could make such a difference, but it really does. We were told to write our goal or vision down and look at it once a week.

Having a plan and writing it down is something God came up with long before anyone else did. It's scriptural to write down the plan God gives you. God told Habakkuk to write down the vision from God. It's amazing, but when you write it down and look at it every week, it keeps you focused and heading in the right direction.

Talk About It

Let your vision come out of your mouth. Jesus told us in Mark 11:23 that we would have whatsoever we say. Begin to declare it! Talk about your dream with those you trust. Say it aloud. Because, remember, we shall have whatsoever we say. (Mark 11:23.)

Proverbs 18:21 tells us that "death and life are in the power of the tongue." The piece of beef between your gums, what is that? That's life or death. You choose to bring either life or death by the words you let come out of your mouth.

When you first start talking about your dream, it may take a few times of saying it before you feel comfortable with it. It may sound too big at first to talk about, and you might feel a little embarrassed to tell others because it seems like something too big for you. But that's okay. God likes to give us dreams that are bigger than we are so He can show us His miracle power. Besides that, if it's not bigger than you are, you're likely to try to do it in your own strength and get into pride. That doesn't help the kingdom of God.

When I hear one of the dreams in my heart come out of my mouth for the first time, I'll think, *Whoa! Did that come out of my mouth?* I start to think about how big it sounds, then insecurities and inadequacies start to rise up in me. I wonder how it can really happen. But then I remember that the Bible says that God is "able to do exceedingly abundantly above all that we ask or think" (Eph. 3:20).

Your dream should be big. It should shock some people who hear it. We have a BIG God who wants to do BIG things in us, through us, and for us. If you don't think your dream is that big a deal, that tells me you're not asking big enough and you're not thinking big enough. God wants us to dream BIG.

Be Careful With Whom You Share Your Dream

Talk about your dream, but be careful when you begin to share your dreams with other people. There are some people who will take that little baby—that vision still so little and fresh and tender—and cause you to abort it. They can look at you funny and talk you right out of giving birth to the dream God put in you. Not everyone is a dreamer. Not everyone will catch hold of your vision with you. Some will get cynical, patronize you, and belittle the whole thing before it has had a chance to grow strong in you. If you're not careful—if you don't keep your heart guarded—all their doubts can jump into you and cause you to postpone, or worse yet, abort that dream.

Before you share your dream with someone, take a moment to stop and check your heart. Use wisdom, because some won't be able to handle that vision and will plant doubt in your heart that will cause you to limit God. Don't let that happen.

You will learn which people not to share your dream with. God will bring people into your path who will encourage you and cause you to dream more. That will bump you up a little higher and get you further up the path to your dream. These are the people who will be valuable to the development and success of your dream.

If I'm going to share a vision with someone, I make sure it's someone I know is a visionary. In fact, I look for people who are even bigger visionaries than I am.

I remember when we moved to the Tulsa area years ago—before we started pastoring in Broken Arrow—we attended another church in the area. One of the first things I did before I ever hooked up with that church was to sit down with the pastor and say, "Pastor, one day I really want to pastor a church. That's in my heart and also in my wife's heart. It's so real to us and it burns in us. I know that's going to be the next step we take. I really love your church and I believe in what you're doing."

That pastor put his arm around me and said, "That's great, Eastman. Do what's in your heart. But, while you're here, would you just plug in with us?"

I thought, *Man, that's wonderful. He's kingdom-minded.*

The day came when God began to stir our hearts to start our own church. I took my pastor out to lunch and remember wondering how he was going to handle it when I told him we were leaving to plant a church. By this time, I knew his heart and that he has one motive: souls. He's kingdom-minded, and I thank God for people like that.

As I began to share my plans with him, he just shook his head with a smile, looked at me, and said, "Eastman, who am I to stop what God has placed in your heart? You need to go after it. You need to do it with everything you've got. If it's God, it's gonna fly. If it isn't God, it is going to fall flat. But who am I to say what is God's will for you?" He smiled really big and said, "Go for it, Eastman!" That's how all of us need to be. Thank God for people who don't have ulterior motives. Find someone you can trust and talk about your dream.

The Bible gives us a good example of this with Moses. In Exodus 4, Moses received specific instructions from God during the supernatural meeting at the burning bush. God Almighty spoke and gave him a mandate to bring the children of God out of Egypt. (Ex. 3:10.) The first thing Moses did was tell someone he trusted: his father-in-law, Jethro. Thank God for spiritual father-in-laws!

Look at what he does in Exodus 4:18. "So Moses went and returned to Jethro his father-in-law, and said to him, 'Please let me go and return to my brethren who are in Egypt, and see whether they are still alive.'" Now, God has told Moses to do it, but here he is asking his father-in-law for permission. He's submissive. So, in Exodus 4:18, Jethro says, "Go in peace." Go, he tells him. Go after it with blessings. Go after it in peace. Go after what God has put in your heart. Thank God for those who will look at the big picture rather than how it's going to affect them personally.

Once your dream is established in your heart, you can tell it to anyone. I remember the night we were about to start the very first service at our church here in Broken Arrow, Oklahoma. A man walked up to me and said, "Eastman, what are you doing? Are you going to start services here in Broken Arrow? They don't need another church in Broken Arrow. What are you doing?"

If he had been the first person that I shared my dream with, his words could have caused me to abort it. But, thank God, he wasn't the first man I shared it with. It was already happening. It was done. It was solidified in my heart. So I just smiled real big and told this man, "Listen, God has called me to do this. I'm going to do it with everything I have. I'm not holding back. I'm taking a step into it."

Sometimes we need to blast through insecurity, become kingdom-minded, and walk in the confidence God has. We need to dream dreams like we've never dreamed before, because there are some things that have never been done before that need to be accomplished in the kingdom of God. And, if we really believe that "all things are possible to him who believes" (Mark 9:23), we can be confident that God will enable us to do all things through Christ Jesus who strengthens us. (Phil. 4:13.) But we can't risk limiting ourselves, so we have to be careful when and with whom we share our dreams.

Keep It Burning

The third thing you need is to let the vision burn in you. Many people skip this step. This is the proving ground. Anyone can obtain a vision, and anyone can write it down, but it takes a person of faith to maintain a vision.

We need to keep that fire, that zeal, alive in us. We need to maintain it and feed it so we don't lose it. It's so sad when you see some people get all fired up about their dream, but then, after a few months or years, they have become complacent or moved in another direction. Their fire has gone out.

That's why it's important to surround yourself with people of faith, people who believe in you and in your vision, people who can build you up in the Lord and encourage you to keep that dream stirred up. There are some people who will believe in you even more than you believe in yourself! Surround yourself with those kinds of people.

So, what are some practical things you can do to keep the fire burning?

A. Encourage yourself in the Lord.

As good as it is to surround yourself with people of faith, it's still up to you to keep the fire burning. No one can stoke your fire for you. You're the one who has to maintain that vision. You're the one who has to keep that dream alive in your heart.

Paul told Timothy to "stir up the gift of God which is in you" (2 Tim. 1:6). He said, "You stir it up."

When the people around David were so discouraged that they began to blame him, he encouraged himself in the Lord. "And David was greatly distressed; for the people spake of stoning him, because the soul of all the people was grieved, every man for his sons and for his daughters: but David encouraged himself in the Lord his God" (1 Sam. 30:6 KJV).

There are times when you can't count on anyone to encourage you. So, if you want to keep your vision alive and burning, you're going to have to learn to encourage yourself in the Lord as David did. Keep stretching and continue to work your faith muscles so you can grow more than you've ever grown before.

I'm just radical enough to believe that it's okay to be more on fire today than you were at the beginning of your faith walk. I know my fire burns stronger now than when I first was saved. One of the first things people told me after I got saved was, "Eastman, you'll be back to normal in a few days." Well, I am not ever going to be "normal" again! I'm a peculiar person and getting more peculiar every day! God has called us to be different. He's called us to be "a chosen generation, a royal priesthood, an holy nation, a peculiar people" (1 Peter 2:9 KJV). It's okay to be different. Be what God called you to be.

B. Watch what you say about your dream.

Your words can make you or break you. Don't let your own words be a snare to your success. (Prov. 6:2.) Guard against the temptation to speak discouragement or failure or doubt over your dream. "Well, I don't know if I can really do this. I'm just a nobody." Stop it! You are not a nobody!

You're a child of God with a spectacular dream! If He called you and designed you to do it, don't you think He'll enable you to do it? "All things are possible to him who believes" (Mark 9:23).

Another thing that dwindles the fire within us is when we belittle our dream. We can't belittle what God has given us. We can't compare it with what He has given others to do. They cannot do what you are called to do the way you can, and you cannot do what they are called to do the way they can. So speak good things about your dream. Hold your head high and rejoice in the purpose God has for you, because it's tailor-made just for you, and that's where you're going to have the most success and the most fun.

C. Keep pursuing your dream.

It's really important to keep pursuing your dream, even when it's slow going, even when it's hard and there are all kinds of opportunities for discouragement. Keep on heading for that destiny. Don't stop at one or two steps. Keep going! And don't look back. The Bible says that "God...is a rewarder of those who diligently seek Him" (Heb. 11:6). Your payday is coming. God will reward you, so don't stop working.

There was a time in the earlier years of our ministry when my wife and I wondered if our payday would ever come. We had been so frustrated because we'd been pushing and pushing and pushing for so long, and it just seemed to be a lot of hard work. We had been in labor a long time! But we knew God's promise that our payday would come. The rewards and blessings were piling up.

So many times we set our hand to the plow and then wonder, *Man, am I the only one out here? What's going on? Am I the only one really fighting for this stuff?* You can feel all alone. But if you stay at it, if you keep pursuing your dream and keep walking the walk and talking the talk, I promise you, your payday is coming!

I'm not only talking about our heavenly reward. When we get to heaven, we will hear Jesus say, "Well done, good and faithful servant." Not only will you receive rewards in the sweet by and by, but God also has rewards for you in the here and now. He has blessings for you here on earth.

Jesus says in Mark 10:29, "Assuredly, I say to you, there is no one who has left house (singular) or brothers or sisters or father or mother or wife or children or lands, for My sake and the gospel's...." He is not talking about forsaking them. He is not saying you have to desert everyone to accomplish the will of God.

He's talking about making it your first priority to fulfill what God has placed in your heart to do. He's talking about how we need to "seek first the kingdom of God and His righteousness, and all these things shall be added to [us]" (Matt. 6:33). But there's a price that we pay to fulfill what God has called us to do. There are sacrifices we will have to make.

Mark 10:30 tells us that those who do this shall "receive a hundredfold." Does it say we'll "receive a hundredfold when we get to heaven"? No. It says there's no one who's done this "who shall not receive a hundredfold now in this time." Notice what He says in the rest of verse 30. Those who forsake these things for the sake of the gospel shall receive a hundredfold back in "houses." Not a house, like the house he left in verse 29. Houses! "...and brothers and sisters and mothers and children and lands...." Then He adds, "with persecutions." Don't you wonder why He stuck that in there?

I'm thinking, *I was just getting fired up, God. You are telling me I am going to receive a hundred times all this great stuff, and then You say 'with persecutions.'* But do you know why He said that? When you start pursuing your dream, persecution is going to come. When you start fulfilling what God has called you to do, there will be some opposition. But keep pursuing your dream, and know that payday is coming. Sometimes it can take a little longer than you'd prefer, but don't you give up. "Though it tarries, wait for it; because it will surely come" (Hab. 2:3).

I remember one New Year's Eve celebration at our church. The auditorium was packed full of people, lights were spinning, and everyone was celebrating the goodness of God. The children were all up at the front, and the whole place was ringing with the sound of the people singing praises to God. At midnight when balloons were dropped, I looked over at my wife and thought to myself, *This is our payday. This is what we've been waiting for. This is only the beginning. We have not seen anything yet compared to what God has.*

We waited, and now we're seeing the rewards come. It's so exciting to see what God is doing.

But we've also found out about that persecution part Jesus mentioned. Along with all the people who are blessed by our ministry and televison shows, we get mail from those who only seek to criticize. People criticize all kinds of funny things. They criticize the way I look and the way I smile all the time. The Bible says that persecutions will come.

It also says, "Blessed are you when they revile and persecute you, and say all kinds of evil against you falsely for My sake" (Matt. 5:11). You'll have attacks against you while you're heading for your dream. Jesus told us they'd come, but it's all worth it; because along with the persecution comes the hundredfold return. With all the criticism and rough spots, we receive the blessings of God and see lives changed.

You need to purpose in your heart to go after your dream, to set your sail for all that God has in store for you. Write the vision down, let it to come out of your mouth, and keep it burning within you. And don't let anyone, any circumstance, any discouragement, or anything else throw you off course.

Chapter 5

Advancing in Your Destiny

Once you have discovered your destiny, have dared to launch out into something new, and have decided to take action, you have to keep advancing in that direction. This can be the hardest part, because there are so many things that can pull you off course or tempt you to quit. You must make a decision to just keep going, even when it gets tough.

> Do not cast away your confidence, which has great reward.
>
> HEBREWS 10:35

Did you know that it takes confidence to move in your destiny? You can't move forward if you don't believe you can. Some people think that confidence is not godly. They associate it with pride or arrogance. Confidence is not the same thing as arrogance. Arrogance is trust in our own human abilities alone. It's when we put confidence in our own flesh.

The Word of God tells us that we're to "have no confidence in the flesh" (Phil. 3:3). But Paul tells us in this same book to be "confident of this very thing, that He who has begun a good work in you will complete it until the day of Jesus Christ" (Phil. 1:6). This is where our confidence is to be. We are to be confident that "He who has begun a good work in [us] will complete it." As we are confident in Christ who is in us, we will move out in the ability He has put in us to accomplish the dream He has given us.

Acts 28:31 says that Paul got on with the work God had given him to do, and he went about "preaching the kingdom of God and teaching the things which concern the Lord Jesus Christ with all confidence." Godly confidence comes from knowing who you are in Christ and what you can accomplish with Him. It's having confidence in God's ability in you. This is essential in order to progress in your destiny.

God Created You for Success

God doesn't see you as a failure. He created you to succeed. "Beloved, I wish above all things that thou mayest prosper and be in health, even as thy soul prospereth" (3 John 2 KJV). The Lord delights to see you prosper. (Ps. 35:27; Deut. 30:9.)

> This Book of the Law shall not depart from your mouth, but you shall meditate in it day and night, that you may observe to do according to all that is written in it. For then you will make your way prosperous, and then you will have good success.
>
> JOSHUA 1:8

I want you to notice something in this Scripture. There are four things which God tells Joshua to do in order to succeed in his destiny. First, he needs to keep the Word of God in his mouth. Second, he is to meditate or think on God's Word continually. Third, he is to choose what he observes. And fourth, he is to do what God says. If we follow this command, we, too, will succeed.

1. Moving Forward With Your Mouth

When you're talking about your dream, it's very important that you use words of faith. Many times people will say, "Oh, brother, I'm praying in faith. I believe that I receive in the name of Jesus. I thank You, God, for Your anointing. I thank You for the financial breakthrough I have been praying for. I believe I receive it. Thank You, Lord!"

But then, as soon as they finish a prayer in faith, they turn around and the first words out of their mouth are, "Oh man, things are really bad. We're really in trouble here. We're all out of money and we're in deep. What are we gonna do? Oh man, how are we ever gonna get out of this mess?"

You cannot pray one way and then talk another way and expect results. If you are going to believe God, let the belief come out of your mouth. You have to use words of faith if you want to go forward. I can't stress this enough. You must keep your faith lined up with your words. Don't let your words keep you from fulfilling your dream.

Proverbs 6:2 warns us about this: "You are snared by the words of your own mouth; you are taken by the words of your mouth." Don't be taken by the enemy because of the words you speak. Did you know that your words can literally hold you captive if you allow them to? You hear some people say things like, "Well, I don't know why everything is going wrong. I always say, if it weren't for bad luck, I'd have no luck at all." And people laugh at that. Don't laugh. Refuse to allow those words to come out of your mouth because they can snare your future! God has something better for you than that!

All you have to do is grab hold of the promises of God and declare them by faith. Let them come out of your mouth. As you begin to do that, you're going to see the anointing of God released in your life.

If you don't like where you are today, it's most likely the result of the words you said yesterday. But the good news is that you can change where you're going to be tomorrow by the words you declare today. Keep words of faith flowing out of your mouth. Declare, "I've got a great future in Jesus' name. God has something extraordinary for me to do. God has good things for me! God has good success for me. God has blessings for me."

Your Words Affect Your Relationships

Do you know that you can literally hold your marriage and family captive and keep them from receiving breakthroughs as a result of the words you speak over them? Sometimes I hear a wife say things like, "All my husband does is sit on the couch all day and flick the remote control. The only exercise he gets is moving that thumb up and down, up and down. That's all he does. He won't accomplish anything. He won't ever have anything."

She has surrounded her husband with words that will hold him captive. Husbands, in turn, can become upset with their wives and say things like, "My wife just sits around at home all day, and, when I get home, all she wants to do is complain. All she does all day is watch the kids. She thinks that's work. She squeezes the toothpaste from the middle, then gets mad at me if I leave the toilet seat up!" He has surrounded her with words of death.

Instead, make a decision to speak words of life. You may have to declare them by faith. You may not see them happening right away, but keep speaking those words of life. When you see your husband just sitting there like a lump on the couch, walk up with a big grin on your face, look at him, and see in faith the man of God he is. Say, "Oh, he's got destiny all over him! My! There's a world-changer right there! He's making the devil nervous all right! That's my man of destiny! Praise God for this godly man!" Declare the Word of God over him. Choose to speak words of life, not death.

Husbands, this is for you too. Declare the Word of the Lord over your wife. "Oh, what a godly woman I'm blessed with. She's always such a blessing to me. She works hard to keep this home running well. She's so efficient. She keeps the house clean. She's such a great mother and a woman of God! She loves the Lord with all her heart. What a blessing she is!" Don't wait until you see it before you start talking it. You've got to say it before you see it.

The same power that joined you with Jesus Christ is the same power that joins you together as husband and wife. Respect that and treat your spouse and others the way you'd like to be treated.

> For assuredly, I say to you, whoever says to this mountain, "Be removed and be cast into the sea," and does not doubt in his heart, but believes that those things he says will be done, he will have whatever he says.
>
> MARK 11:23

Notice that Jesus talks about "saying" three times in this verse, and He mentions "believing" only once. What does that tell you? We need to declare our faith. I've met people who say, "Just believe. That's all you have to do. Just believe and everything's going to be okay." No. You also have to line your words up with your faith. Jesus Christ said that you would have whatever you say. He stressed the saying part three times.

Your words can either be a thermometer or a thermostat. Your words can reinforce what's happening the way a thermometer does, or they can literally change the environment as a thermostat does. The Bible says that the tongue is like a rudder. (James 3:4,5.) It acts like a rudder in a ship, which can change the direction of the whole ship. You can change the course of your destiny by the words of your mouth. You can turn your whole life around by the words you speak. Use your tongue for good and not for evil, and you will see the power of God released in your life.

Earlier I mentioned the television evangelist scandals. The whole United States was airing their dirty laundry because they were such big ministries. I began to think about how this would affect the rest of us in ministry. One day I said to my wife, "Tough times are coming, honey. It's going to be tough. People won't be giving to evangelists after this because they're going to be really skeptical. We need to get ready because tough times are coming." And they came! We weren't able to pay our bills, and things backed up. It was really tough—just like I said it would be.

I blamed it all on what had happened with other ministries and people's fear to trust evangelists. I got on my face before God and said, "Lord, do You want me to do something else? Am I in the wrong business? Do You want me to go get another job? Just tell me what to do and I'll do it. Apparently, something is wrong and I need to understand what it is."

Then the Spirit of God spoke to me, *Eastman, the problem is with you and that big ol' tongue flapping between your gums.*

Suddenly, I realized what had happened. I remembered what Jesus said about how we will have whatever we say. And, boy, had I been saying the wrong things! I'd enforced it with my own tongue.

I asked my wife to help me. Give a woman a job to do, and she's going to help you. I said, "Honey, I want you to help me with my confession. I need your help to speak positive words, because I am the one who dug this hole we are in. I've been declaring that no one's going to be giving to our ministry, and now we've got just what I said. Well, maybe I dug myself into this hole, but we're getting out of this thing."

You would be wise to watch what you say.

Beware of Old Habits

Right after that revelation, I decided to really seek the Lord for direction in our ministry. I went into my prayer room and got on my face before God. When I came out, my wife, Angel, looked at me and said with this big grin on her face, "Oh, man of God, did you hear from the Lord? Do you know where we're going?"

I just looked at her and said, "Oh, honey, I've been seeking God, but I haven't got anything from the Lord. I've been praying and praying. All I'm getting is confused. I don't know what direction we are going in. It's been hard for me to hear from God. I don't know what's happening."

All the while my wife kept grinning from ear to ear and shaking her head up and down. Then she—being the great helpmate she is—said, "Honey, I tell you what. I agree with every word that's coming out of your mouth. You don't hear from God. You're so confused. You don't know what direction to go in. It's hard for you to hear from God."

Angel helped me to see the negative words I had been speaking. I decided to turn that thing around right then. "Oh, I repent! I'm sorry! You're right! Oh, God, I do hear Your voice. The voice of a stranger I will not follow." (John 10:4,5.) I began to quote the Scriptures and turn them into confessions of faith. "'As many as are led by the Spirit of God, they're the sons of God' (Rom. 8:14). I'm God's son, and I am led by the Spirit of God." I became fired up about it, and before that afternoon was over, I knew exactly what direction I needed to go by the Spirit of God!

Sometimes we fall into habits and don't even realize what we are saying. These are habits you must break—before they break you!

It all begins with the words of your mouth. What are you saying? If you don't like where you are today, begin to charge the atmosphere with faith. Fill the atmosphere with words of life.

A friend of mine pastors a church in Syracuse, New York. I have talked to many in the evangelistic fields who have told me, "Never go to upstate New York. It's a preacher's graveyard up there. There is no move of God there. People aren't hungry for God there."

But my pastor friend called me and said, "Eastman, you have to come to our church! It's growing. It's exploding! You'd love it. People are growing there."

"You're kidding," I said. I had never heard anyone talk about upstate New York like this.

"Yeah, it's really something. You've gotta come and see it."

So, I went there, and, sure enough, his church is vibrant. It's growing. It's exciting. People are being born again and filled with the Holy Spirit. It is just as he said.

When he and I went out to lunch, I said, "What's going on here? I've talked to so many people and they've all said this is a graveyard up here."

He looked at me and grinned. "You know why it's a graveyard for them? Because that's what they're saying. But I purposed in my heart that this was going to be easy and fun. We will have revival, and if anyone's going to have a move of God, it might as well be us. I started proclaiming that over the people, and look what God is doing!"

It's really amazing to see what's happening up there. He built a beautiful facility and the church is growing, but it started with the attitude of his heart and the words of his mouth.

2. *Changing Your Course With Your Thoughts*

One of the greatest revelations I ever received was when I realized that I'm the one in control of my thought life. I remember one time shortly after I got saved, when I was sitting in church and a very negative picture popped into my head. There I was, saved, baptized in the Holy Spirit, and right in the middle of the church service, when this terrible picture steamrolled over my mind. *Oh God,* I thought, *I don't want to think that thought.* The devil started in on me: *Look at you, thinking a thought like that! And in the house of God.* I felt guilty, condemned, and beat up about the whole thing. Then the enemy said, *You can't be a Christian. No Christian would ever think a thought like that—and in church! Tsk, tsk. Thinking a thought like that! Shame on you.*

What I didn't understand was just because we have a thought flash through our mind, does not mean we're no longer saved. The devil can bring thoughts to our mind, but that doesn't mean we have to let them stay there. Just because you have a bad thought doesn't mean you have to dwell on it. If you dwell on it and keep dwelling on it, it's going to grab hold of you and lead you right into sin. It's not the thoughts themselves that are the sin. It's what you do with those thoughts that determine if you will sin or not.

When the pastor gave an altar call for people to be saved, I jumped out of my seat and ran up to the front. I knew I couldn't be saved, because no Christian would ever have that kind of thought! When I reached the altar, I prayed and cried. I felt so bad. And that wasn't the first time I did that. I can't tell you how many times I responded to an altar call to be born again.

I must have gotten "born again" again and again and again. The problem wasn't that I needed to be saved over and over again. The problem was that I needed to understand some things about my thought life. I needed to understand that God had given me the ability to take control of my thought life and to renew my mind.

Romans 12:1-2 says, "I beseech you therefore, brethren, by the mercies of God, that you present your bodies a living sacrifice, holy, acceptable to God, which is your reasonable service. And do not be conformed to this world, but be transformed by the renewing of your mind, that you may prove what is that good and acceptable and perfect will of God."

I like the New Living Translation of verse 2: "Don't copy the behavior and customs of this world, but let God transform you into a new person by changing the way you think."

God wants to change us into brand-new people. He wants us to change from defeat to victory, failure to success, discouragement to strength, bondage to freedom. God wants us to succeed and be victorious. Victory comes through the renewal of our mind. When our mind is renewed, we think and see ourselves differently. We envision good things happening in our lives. As we transform our minds, we each become the person God always meant for us to be.

Renewing your mind is an ongoing process. The same way we learn and grow in the natural is the way we learn and grow in the spiritual. The more we spend time reading God's Word, the more our minds are renewed. The more time we spend delighting in the Lord, the more our minds become like His.

Fight for Your Thought Life

> For though we walk in the flesh, we do not war according to the flesh. For the weapons of our warfare are not carnal but mighty in God for pulling down strongholds, casting down arguments and every high thing that exalts itself against the knowledge of God, bringing every thought into captivity to the obedience of Christ.
>
> 2 CORINTHIANS 10:3-5

What does it mean when it refers to "pulling down strongholds"? A lot of people have interpreted "strongholds" to mean demonic powers from which we need to be delivered. But if you look at the whole context of this verse, you'll see that it refers to what's in our minds.

Webster's dictionary defines *stronghold* as "a place having strong defenses; fortified place; a place where a group having certain views, attitudes, etc. is concentrated."[1] Many times we build strongholds in our mind because of continual thought patterns. For example, if you think, *I'll never succeed, I just always mess up, I can't do anything right, God can never use me,* then you're building a stronghold of negative thoughts in your mind.

Our minds are places where we hold our views, attitudes, and beliefs. When our minds are not renewed to the truth of God's Word, many of these old views, attitudes, beliefs, and thought patterns can be like a wall we need to pull down.

When Paul says we're to pull down these strongholds, he's giving us a picture of a battle. There used to be fortresses around cities. So, when one city (or kingdom) attacked another, the soldiers would work to pull down the fortress, or stronghold, of their enemy. That's how they won the battle.

The battlefield of your mind is where you have to fight for your thought life.

Second Corinthians 10:5 says, "Casting down arguments...." Arguments come from our minds. Verse 5 goes on to say, "...and every high thing that exalts itself against the knowledge of God bringing every thought into captivity to the obedience of Christ." The battle begins in our mind. Therefore, we need to learn to fight for our thought life and bring it under the control of the Holy Spirit.

We Are the Ones Who Control Our Thoughts

We have to pull down the strongholds of lies from the enemy and fill our minds with the truth of God's Word. We have been given control over our thought life because of the anointing and power of the Holy Spirit given us by God. Self-control is a fruit of the Holy Spirit. (Gal. 5:23.) He gave you the ability to bring every thought into captivity to the obedience of Christ.

Every time a thought that contradicts the Word of God comes to our minds, we must replace it with something positive—the truth of God's Word. If a lustful thought pops into your head, don't just sit there and flirt with it or feel condemned. Put your foot down as a child of God and do what Jesus did when Satan handed Him a temptation. Say, "Get away from me, Satan!"

The Bible is your weapon to defeat the devil with, but if you're going to win the battle, you need to know how to use that weapon. Find out what it says about your situation. The moment a wrong thought pops into your head, get it out of there. Refuse to allow it to settle there. Get rid of it! Take it captive before it has time to get into your mouth.

Choose to keep your thoughts on what God says, not what circumstances or other people or the devil or even your own flesh says. If you don't, you're going to move right into discouragement, fear, and depression. You've got to deal with the wrong thoughts right away so they don't form a strong-hold in your mind.

I wish I could tell you that someone else could change your thoughts for you. But you are the only one who can control your thought life. I can't do it for my wife or kids. I can't do it for my congregation. I can't do it for my readers. God has given us a free will and the ability to choose what we feed our minds. God will help you do what you need to do, but He won't make you do it. It's something you choose to do. Fight for your thought life and win over all the wrong thoughts that try to pull you off course from your destiny.

Once you really understand this, it's going to enable you to blast into new realms and dimensions in faith and with favor. Thinking God's thoughts can launch you into your destiny.

Look at Joshua chapter one. Joshua is just receiving his mandate from God to bring the children of Israel into the Promised Land. When God wanted to deliver the people from Egypt, He had to use someone who wasn't in bondage. He needed someone who was not held captive in Egypt. He needed someone who didn't have all the limitations of a slave mentality. He called Moses to do the job. Moses was brought up in Pharaoh's house, so he didn't think like a slave. So many times we limit God and ourselves by our own thinking.

When it was time for Moses to move on to heaven, God chose Joshua to bring the people into the promises of God. Joshua was a man who would not limit God. He knew enough to hang around Moses, the man who believed that all things are possible with God. Joshua was with Moses long enough to see firsthand some of the things God could do.

Like Moses, Joshua didn't place limits on God but moved as God led. The anointing that was on Moses was transferred to Joshua.

When you spend time with believers, it helps you to be a better believer. Time spent with dreamers will cause you to dream. Possibility thinkers cause you to realize all things are possible. That's why it's so important to choose relationships that will keep you going in the right direction. The people we open our hearts to and let our guard down with can either lead us into captivity or liberty. Choose liberty.

It is important to understand what belongs to you. Success is something God desires for you to have. It's good, and it belongs to you. Don't let the devil steal your success. Some people argue that Jesus was poor, so they think you should follow His example. Jesus became poor so that through His poverty we would be made rich. The Bible says He redeemed us from the curse of the Law. (Gal. 3:13.) And poverty is as much a part of the curse as sickness and disease. So don't let one blessing slip through your fingers. Grab hold of the promises of God and get everything that belongs to you.

Train Your Mind To Operate at a Higher Level

When I was a boy, my dad owned a tourist attraction business with all kinds of wild animals. There was a man in charge of all the animals who taught me what to do if I was ever attacked by one of them. There were different things you had to do, depending on which kind of animal was involved or what was going on. If a bobcat bit you, for instance, you were supposed to handle it differently than if a bear bit you.

I remember when I was eight years old, I was feeding a big black bear we had. His name was Toby. We raised him from a cub, but he was still wild. While I was shoveling some dog food into his cage, some of the food fell on the ground outside of his cage. I scooped it up and was throwing it to the other side of the cage, when Toby flew toward me with lightning speed and, with one swoop, reached through the bars, grabbed my hand, and drew it into his mouth.

As I stood there with my hand in this bear's mouth, it seemed as if everything went into slow motion. I remembered what this man had taught me to do. "If a bear ever bites you," he'd told me, "don't pull back." Your mind thinks, *Pull your hand out; pull it out!* But that's not what you're supposed to do. You have to do just the opposite of what your mind's telling you to do. "If a bear bites you," he said, "shove your hand right down his throat." The bear will gag and automatically regurgitate your hand.

Immediately I jammed my hand down that bear's throat—and he spit it out. When I did that, it saved my hand. If I had not known that, I would not have my hand today.

Sometimes we have to do the same thing with the thoughts that attack us. Don't let the devil eat up your dream or chew up your children, health, prosperity, or success. Don't let him pull you into wrong thinking and negative confessions. You just shove those things right back down his throat!

When your thought life is under attack, remember what the Word says to do.

In order to walk in victory, you must train your mind to think in line with the Word of God. Choose to think on what's good and right and noble and true. Philippians 4:8 tells us to do this:

Whatever things are true, whatever things are noble, whatever things are just, whatever things are pure, whatever things are lovely, whatever things are of good report, if there is any virtue and if there is anything praiseworthy—meditate on these things.

Meditate on these things. Don't meditate on the negative things. Don't think about the bad report. Don't dwell on all the things you don't like about a person. Focus on their strengths. The same goes for how you think about yourself. Don't focus on your weaknesses, but think about the gifts God has given you. Consider the blessings He has poured out on you and the great dream He has given you.

I love positive thinkers. I love to hear optimists talking. "I just got fired last week, but, praise God! I know He has a better job for me! I'm gonna go get me the job of my dreams! Hallelujah!"

I heard a story about twins who were complete opposites. Although they were brought up in the same home, raised by the same family, went to the same school, and attended the same church, they were completely different. One was an optimist, and the other was a pessimist. This really baffled psychologists, so they ran all types of tests on the twins. In one test, they put thousands of dollars' worth of toys in a room. They put the pessimist in the room and told him, "You can play with any toy you want to."

You might think this would be heaven for any kid, but this little pessimist started bawling just three minutes after they put him in this room. With closed circuit TV, they saw him sitting on the floor, tears streaming down his face, just sobbing like the world had ended. One of the psychologists ran into the room to see what was wrong. "There's too many toys in here!" the kid said. "I don't know which one to play with."

That is a typical pessimist. You would think he could find something good in that room, but he focused on the negative.

Next they tested the other twin, the one who was optimistic about every-thing. They determined the worst environment to put this kid in would be a floor covered with about a foot of manure. Then they put this little opti-mist in there. "You're going to be in there a while," they told him as they shoved him in, "so get used to it." Within two minutes they saw this kid on camera spinning around, singing, dancing, shouting, laughing, picking up manure, flinging it around, and spinning some more. He was having a blast! He's covered from head to toe with manure and just giggling. So the psychologists went in and asked, "What's going on? What are you doing?"

The little boy looked up at them with a big grin and said, "With all this horse manure, I know there's a pony under here somewhere!"

That's the kind of attitude we all need to have. When you're knee deep in poop, just keep looking for the pony!

Fix your eyes on what is good and true and noble and just. Think on what is pure and lovely and praiseworthy. Think about the good report and fix your thoughts on whatever is of any virtue. Meditate on these things.

As a Man Thinketh, So Is He

"For as he thinketh in his heart, so is he" (Prov. 23:7 KJV).

Before I ever ask God for anything, I like to go to His Word. The Bible tells us that, when we pray, we need to pray believing that we have received what we've asked for. (Matt. 21:22.) But if you're going to do that, the first thing you need to do is tank up with the Word of God. There have been times when I've asked God for something before I was really ready to see it happen in my heart. So I'd ask Him, but then I'd begin to falter in my faith. Now I've learned to go to the Word of God, find the promises there for what I'm asking, then meditate on that Word until it becomes real to me. When it's burning in my heart, I pray believing that I have received it.

I know it's mine. I may not see it with my physical eyes, but I see it in the spirit. I know I'm asking in faith.

It has to start with us. It starts right on the inside of our hearts. When we see it in our hearts, we can have it.

3. What You See Is What You Get

How do you see yourself? Do you see yourself as just barely getting by? Or do you see yourself prospering and succeeding? Do you see yourself moving in the destiny God has for you? Do you see yourself winning thousands of people to the Lord and operating in the fullness of all that God has for you? Whatever you can see in the spirit is what you'll get.

Sometimes we need to get a new vision. We need to get rid of that old mental Polaroid of ourselves and take a brand-new one. We need to see ourselves as God sees us: blessed coming in, blessed going out (Deut. 28:6), blessed in everything we do. See yourself as prosperous. See everything you touch prospering. You need to see that happening. As you begin to see it, it is going to happen, and that is the way you are going to go. But you have to see it first. See yourself achieving. See yourself advancing in your destiny. See yourself obtaining all that God has for you.

There are some people who will never prosper because they're afraid of success. The reason they're afraid of it is because of how they view themselves. They don't see themselves prospering. There are some who can't see themselves being successful. When they get into a position where things are starting to go right and it looks like they are getting close to success, they will end up doing something that causes their faith to shipwreck. They will sabotage their own victory. Subconsciously, they are afraid to be successful.

I knew a man with all the potential in the world. But as soon as things started going his way, he would throw a wrench in it. He goofed up because his heart was not enlarged to where he could actually embrace success. He couldn't see himself as successful.

No one has to stay there. I've been in touch with him since then, and he is reading the Word of God. He participates in Bible studies, listens to tapes I send him, and is enlarging his heart and preparing for success. I recently talked to him by phone, and I can tell he has grown. He's ready now. He sees himself as successful. He sees himself being able to prosper. So now he'll be able to do it.

It starts with the way that you see yourself.

Look at Joshua 1:8 KJV again: "For then thou shalt make thy way prosperous, and then thou shalt have good success."

Notice that the Word says, "good success." Success is good. God calls success good! A lot of people think that success is bad because religious tradition and some false teaching have said this. So people think, *God wants me to barely get through life. If I can just get through and walk through those portals of heaven, that is all that matters.* But that's not true. That's not what the Word of God tells us. Jesus told us that He came not only to give us life, but to give it to us more abundantly. (John 10:10.) God not only wants you to have an abundant entrance into heaven, but to have abundance here on earth. We need abundance to accomplish the will of God. We need an abundance of health and energy and money and supplies and provision. Abundance is good. It's God's idea. And success is God's idea too.

The devil will fight you over your prosperity and your healing. He'll even take Scriptures and twist them to your disadvantage. But God wants you to walk in health. He wants you healed, and He wants you to prosper and succeed. God wants you to have more than enough to get by—not just to have things for yourself and your dream, but so that you can be a blessing to others.

Never Be Ashamed of Success

When we first started traveling in ministry, we had a little car. We'd go from place to place in that little car, and by the time we'd get to where we were going, we'd still be vibrating from the way it shook. We'd get out and be half-whipped and worn to the bone. So after a while, my wife said to me, "Honey, we really need to believe God for a motor home. Let's believe God for something nice." So that's what we did. We started grabbing hold of the Word of God and putting prosperity Scriptures on little three-by-five cards and sticking them on the refrigerator. We'd see Scriptures in the mirror every morning. We'd pull the visor down in the car and a Scripture would fall out. We had them duct-taped everywhere.

The more we filled our minds and hearts with the Word, the more real they became to us. Eventually God supernaturally blessed us with a $130,000 motor home. We got it for $40,000. It was a true miracle. This was in the mid-80s, so a $130,000 motor home was really something then. It was beautiful. It surpassed my wildest imagination. It had a skylight in the bathroom, two separate entertainment centers, a queen-sized bed, a water purifier, and an all-oak interior. It had everything I could dream of and things I had never even imagined.

After that, when we were traveling on the road, we would arrive at our destination and no longer feel all beat up. One of us could take a nap while the other drove. We could make meals while we were driving. And we'd be refreshed and invigorated by the time we got to our destination. What a blessing!

One time we pulled into a church parking lot with this motor home, and I didn't want the people to see us with it because it was too nice. I was afraid they would think I was too successful. I didn't think they'd would like that since I was in the ministry. Some people think that ministers are supposed to barely get by. I found myself parking the motor home miles from the church, unhooking our little old car—complete with all its engine-popping sounds—and driving it to the church. One day I pulled into the church and the pastor asked, "Is this what you travel around in?"

"Well," I reluctantly admitted, "we have a little motor home, and we just parked it and drove over."

Then I found myself making excuses for even having a motor home. That night the Spirit of God rose up inside me and said, *I don't want you to blush. I don't want you to be ashamed of the blessings that I give you. It will encourage other people to tap into what God has for them, because I am no respecter of persons.*

When you see someone blessed, don't fold your arms and pop up your eyebrows like a Klingon from Star Trek. Just grin from ear to ear and say, "Glory to God! If God did it for that person, He can do it for me too!"

So I quit making excuses after that. We'd pull our big blessing up and park right up close. During the service, I talked about the miracle of how God blessed us, and how He could bless them too. Then I'd invite them to come and see our motor home after the service if they wanted to. And, all of a sudden, people started getting a vision to move up in life too.

God wants you blessed so you can be a blessing to others. Some will tell you that you shouldn't have anything to do with the mammon of the world. Don't let that religious thinking attach itself to you. Money is not a bad thing. It is a tool. You can do good with it or you can do evil with it. So do some good with it. God wants you to fund His end-time harvest. And you need money to do it.

Now, don't go to the other extreme. Don't go flaunting all your blessings in front of everyone just to show off. I can remember preaching about prosperity when we were living on $200 a month. That's what we had, but we were still out there preaching the truth: "God wants you to prosper. God wants you blessed." We would see people blessed while we were still strug-gling along. But I kept preaching it, kept declaring it, and kept saying it. We kept sowing, and pretty soon we started seeing it come in.

See Yourself Moving in Your Destiny

One thing I do before I ever step out on a platform to preach is go in a back room and see myself giving an altar call. Before I've preached a word, I've seen hundreds of teenagers running to the altars to be born again. I've seen them with their hands up in the air, sobbing and worshiping God, receiving what God has for them. I've seen them baptized in the Spirit, healed, set free. I see all this before my sermon even starts. I believe this is one of the keys to seeing people become born again and healed in our con-ventions and crusades.

My brother-in-law, Fred, is one of the top insurance salesmen in my father-in-law's insurance company. He's incredible in sales. So one day I asked him, "Fred, you can sell ice to an Eskimo and they'll feel good about buying it from you. How do you do this?"

"Number one," he told me, "I have a product that's going to bless them, and it's going to help people. Many of them don't know that they need it, but they do need it. It can really help them. Another thing I do is, before I ever go out to make one sale, I shut my eyes and see people excited about buying insurance. I see them signing on the bottom line. I see them fired up. I see them not only excited about buying insurance, but giving me referrals for other people who want to buy insurance. That's what I see. I don't roll out of bed and say, 'Oh, I don't know who's going to buy any-thing today. I hope 10 percent of the people I see buy.' I don't do that. I see everyone excited about buying. If someone does not buy insurance, it shocks me, because I have already seen him or her buy it. But, if that happens, I just brush the dust off my feet and go on to the next one who's ready to make that purchase."

The way you look at things will be the difference between your success or failure, happiness or depression. You can look at things in the negative, or you can look at things in the positive. You can see people the way God sees them, or you can see them in a negative light. You can think, *They aren't going to amount to anything.* Or you can think, *Now there's someone who's going to make it.* It's all in how you see it.

You will begin to understand your destiny when you reach out and grab hold of what God has for you. When you understand and believe that God has a special plan and purpose for you to fulfill, it will help you tap into your talent. When God puts a dream in your heart, it not only gives you something to reach for, but it opens the eyes of your heart and enables you to see further and more optimistically than before. When you know God has given you something to do, you start to see it happening. You will see all the provision for that dream coming in. You notice everything working out to help you get there. You see what belongs to you. And you see yourself grabbing hold of it. Study the Word of God. Search out the promises of God for yourself, and see them as yours.

In John 8:56, Jesus says, "Your father Abraham rejoiced to see My day, and he saw it and was glad." Abraham saw the day of Jesus. "Well, how could he see it?" you ask. "He wasn't even born yet." He saw it by faith in his spirit.

Look From the Place Where You Are

Abraham also saw some other things. In Genesis 13:14, the Lord told Abram, "Lift your eyes now and look from the place where you are." God told him to look from the place where he was. Often, we want to wait until we have been saved for decades before we see what God has for us. We want to wait until after we get a financial breakthrough, or until after we get married. No. Look and see what God has for you right now from where you are.

Ask the Holy Spirit to open your spiritual eyes and see it from where you are today. God wants to get involved in your life. But you need to begin to dream right now. Begin to allow the Holy Spirit to paint pictures in your heart through the Word of God. "This Book of the Law shall not depart from your mouth, but you shall meditate in it day and night, that you may observe to do according to all that is written in it" (Josh. 1:8). You have to observe it in order to do it. You have to see it in your heart so that you can get up and do it.

So God said to Abram, "Lift your eyes now and look from the place where you are...for all the land which you see I give to you and your descendants forever" (Gen. 13:14,15). Keep in mind that Abram didn't have any children at this point. His wife was still barren, but God was telling him He had given this land to him and his descendants.

God went on to tell Abram some of the things He was going to do in his life. And Abram saw it. He looked at the land God was showing him, and he saw in his heart that it was his. He saw that God was going to give him a son who would inherit the land after him. By faith Abram saw these things before they ever happened.

Using Your Imagination for God

Abram applied faith to see the promise of God through the imagination God had given him. He saw these things before they happened because he visualized them in his heart.

I can hear some of you thinking that this sounds like New Age teaching. It is not New Age! The idea to visualize things doesn't originate from the devil. He is not an originator but a counterfeiter. He steals from God and twists it to his advantage. He does it all the time. Look at the different cults around the world. They've all taken something of the truth and distorted it.

So what if the New Agers have borrowed the idea of visualization—of seeing things in their hearts before they happen—from Christianity! They have borrowed many other things from Christianity, too. The New Age movement also believes in prayer, but that does not mean we should throw prayer out, too!

Many people in the body of Christ have missed out on releasing their faith and tapping into some of the great things that God has in store for them—all because they're afraid to associate with something another group happens to utilize. If anyone's going to be blessed, it should be us as children of God. If anyone's going to prosper, it ought to be a child of the King of kings.

The Bible says, "The wealth of the sinner is stored up for the righteous" (Prov. 13:22). It's meant for us! It's meant for those of us who have been made the righteousness of God in Christ. (2 Cor. 5:21.) The world has gotten a lot of the wealth for a long time, but that is only because we Christians have let it go to them. They have it because many of us didn't know it belonged to us.

We have to see it, and we can do that as we visualize it in our hearts. We imagine it.

Some people think imagination is from the devil, but it is not. God is a God of creativity. He is the One who placed imagination inside of you, and He wants you to use that imagination for Him. Often people won't use what God has given them because they don't realize it's from God. Imagination is a gift from God, and He desires for us to use it for His glory.

The problem comes when we use our imagination for the wrong things. Why is it so easy to use our imagination for things like fear and doubt and unbelief, but difficult to use it in faith to see good things coming to us? We imagine all kinds of bad things happening to us. We must use our imaginations to picture good things happening, and see ourselves prosperous and successful.

God gave us imagination and a free will, so we choose how we will use our imagination and what we use it for. Realize that it is your world, and it is time for you to make it happen in your life. But you have to see it in your heart before you prove it in your life.

When God told Abram that He was going to make his descendants as abundant as the dust of the earth and the stars in the heavens, Abram saw it. He believed it. He used his imagination to grasp it and to see it. God is the One who wanted Abram to use his imagination to see His will for him. He was the One who told Abram, *I want you to see it, Abram. I want you to see your descendants. Look at the dust and think about how you can't possibly count each particle of dust on the earth, and see how many descendants I'm giving you. I want you to look at the stars of the heaven, Abram, and see how many stars are up there. That's how many descendants you're going to have.* And Abram looked and he saw it. What is that? That's using your imagination for good and not for evil.

When you learn to start using your imagination for good, you're going to see breakthroughs take place in your life. When you start thinking big thoughts for the kingdom of God and start using your imagination for God, that's when you're going to see some changes in your life. That's when you're going to take off for your destiny. That's when God's dream in you is going to become a reality.

It amazes me how the body of Christ can believe God for finances, cars, houses, and all kinds of things, but forget to use their faith for their destiny. Why must we begin to use our imagination to see God's will being done on earth as it is in heaven?

The Bible says that by His stripes you were healed. (1 Peter 2:24.) So what do you do when the doctor says you're not healed? What do you do when the tests say you're still sick? What do you do when you still feel terrible? Are you going to picture yourself getting worse? Or are you going to shut your eyes and see that by the stripes of Jesus you were healed? What are you doing when you do that? You're seeing the Word of God at work within your heart.

What do you do when there just doesn't seem to be a way out of your financial dilemma? Are you going to look at your circumstances and imagine yourself stuck with this problem for the rest of your life? Are you going to imagine yourself getting kicked out of your home because you can't pay the rent?

If you will move into the presence of God, you will begin to see that God has supplied all your needs according to His riches in glory. (Phil. 4:19.)

"He who overcomes shall inherit all things" (Rev. 21:7). Maybe you don't feel like an overcomer. You may look at your life and think you haven't been overcoming at all. Maybe you've seen yourself bound up with fear, unbelief, sexual immorality, pornography, depression, or discouragement. It doesn't have to stay that way. You can change that photograph in your mind today. God wants you to get a new picture of yourself. He wants you to put in some new lenses and start seeing yourself as He sees you. He sees you as an overcomer. He sees His Spirit in you. He sees Jesus in you. And Jesus told us that He has overcome the world. (John 16:33.) That makes you an overcomer.

4. Doing the Word of God

> Be doers of the Word, and not hearers only....
>
> But he who looks into the perfect law of liberty and continues in it, and is not a forgetful hearer but a doer of the work, this one will be blessed in what he does.
>
> JAMES 1:22,25

Once you get your mouth, your thoughts, and the eyes of your heart in line with the Word of God, it's time to act. Some people speak the Word of God over their lives, but then they turn around and act like they never said anything at all. You move into action if you want to move into your destiny. Speak, think, see, and act on the promises of God. God told Joshua to do all that he'd spoken, meditated on, and observed. "For then you will make your way prosperous, and then you will have good success" (Josh. 1:8). That is how he moved into the promises of God. That is how Joshua went into the Promised Land and took what belonged to him.

Look at Genesis 13 again. Abram lifted up his eyes and saw the promises of God. God then told Abram to do something else. "Arise, walk in the land through its length and its width, for I give it to you. Then Abram moved...." (Gen. 13:17,18). Abram got up and moved into his destiny. He saw what God had promised him, and then he got up and went for it.

Speak words of faith over your destiny. Keep your thoughts on what the Word of God says about you and your destiny. See yourself moving successfully in your destiny, and make it happen!

Paul instructs Timothy by saying, "Give yourself entirely to them, that your progress may be evident to all" (1 Tim. 4:15). The King James Version uses the word "profitting." I looked up the word *profitting* in the Greek. It means "to advance, to move forward by continuous hammering."[2] Have you ever seen someone drilling for oil? They use a spiral drill, which is really a pipe being hammered down into the ground. You can hear it making a bumping, grinding sound. The workers keep driving that pipe farther and farther in the ground with continual hammering.

That's how God wants us to be with the destiny He has called us to. He wants us to be persistent with the good success He's destined for us. He wants us to give ourselves entirely to that, and then to keep progressing in our destiny. He wants us to keep moving forward in the calling He's given us.

One time when Angel and I were visiting Mike Francen, an evangelist friend of ours who lived in Miami at the time, we saw a huge photograph he had. It was filled with thousands of people all the way across, so I asked him about it.

"That was an incredible crusade," he told me with a great big happy grin on his face. Then he told me the name of the great man of God who had held this meeting in Africa. "There were over a million people there."

"A million people! That's incredible!" And, as I looked at the picture, I started dreaming a little bit bigger. I could tell that it inspired Mike, too, every time he looked at it. I could see that it was spurring him on to dream bigger. "Man," I looked at him, "that had to be great!"

"Oh, that was a wonderful meeting," he told me, "and it was the largest meeting."

"Really? It didn't get bigger than that?"

"No."

"Why do you think that is?" I asked.

Then Mike told me that something happened after that meeting. When it was over, a certain man of God thought that the meeting was as big as it could ever get, that they had reached as many people as he could ever reach at one time. "And he hasn't had a bigger meeting since," Mike said.

The man backed off from his dreams. After experiencing a huge success, he didn't think it could get better than that and he stopped his pursuit. He no longer advanced but continued to look over his shoulder and say, "I remember when we ran a million people. Remember that one meeting we had? Wasn't that something?"

I don't ever want to get to the place that I stop dreaming and growing. I don't ever want to stop my pursuit for more of God. I don't ever want to get to the point of saying, "Well, praise God! We've arrived. Look at what we've done. Look at all we've accomplished."

When we quit dreaming, something dangerous happens. We begin to take credit for what we've done instead of looking to God for more, and then we stop growing in what God has for us. I don't want to reach that place. I want to keep going forward in the things God has for me. I want to keep the dreams stirred up.

Success is good. God wants us to succeed. But when we let success go to our head, it blocks our progression. When we no longer lean on God and we give ourselves credit for "our" achievements, we are no longer going forward in the plan of God. This places a limit on our success, and, before long, we find that we have stopped dreaming. Our thinking becomes limited and we are unable to see anything better in the future.

Don't limit God. Don't stop dreaming. Continue to advance in the plan of God for you.

Chapter 6

Don't Just Sit There, Do Something!

If you have ever floated down a river in an inner tube, you know how easy it is to just sit in that inner tube and let the current carry you wherever it wants to. You can sit back, dangle your legs over the tubing, and float downstream.

That's the way a lot of Christians are when it comes to their spiritual progress. They just float through life and allow their circumstances to take them wherever they will. "Whatever will be, will be," they sigh. Circumstances toss them about every way but forward. That's not what God wants for you. Ephesians 4:14 tells us "we should no longer be children, tossed to and fro."

Little babies need to be carried, but soon it's time for them to walk. After they learn to walk, they run and leap and dance. That's how God meant for it to be in our spiritual lives as well. It's time for us to leave the inner tube behind and step into God's motorboat so we can push off into our destiny with power. Crank up that 150-horsepower motor, rev up the power of the Holy Spirit, and move in the right direction.

> And there were four leprous men at the entering in of the gate: and they said one to another, Why sit we here until we die?
>
> 2 Kings 7:3 KJV

In this story there are four lepers sitting outside the city gate. Not only are they lepers—which is bad enough—but they're also under siege in the midst of a famine and a drought. Ben Hadad, the king of Syria, has besieged Samaria—which means he had set up a fortress around it and wouldn't let anyone in or out of the city. There is no food and no way to get out to get some. Some of the people are so desperate that they have resorted to cannibalism. Things were rough.

The four lepers sat there discussing their predicament among themselves. "If we say, 'We will enter the city,' the famine is in the city, and we shall die there. And if we sit here, we die also. Now therefore, come, let us surrender to the army of the Syrians. If they keep us alive, we shall live; and if they kill us, we shall only die. And they rose at twilight to go" (2 Kings 7:4,5).

They rose up. In verse 5, the New International Version says, "they got up and went." Often we talk about things, plan things, draw it out on paper, meditate on our plan, and pray about it, but we never get up and do something about it. It's good to think about your plans, confess the Word over them, discuss them, and write them out. But it's when you decide to rise up and go in the direction you know you're supposed to go that it will then produce results.

Notice that the lepers rose at twilight. They did not waste any time.

> And they rose at twilight to go to the camp of the Syrians; and when they had come to the outskirts of the Syrian camp, to their surprise no one was there. For the Lord had caused the army of the Syrians to hear the noise of chariots and the noise of horses—the noise of a great army; so they said to one another, "Look, the king of Israel has hired against us the kings of the Hittites and the kings of the Egyptians to attack us!" Therefore they arose and fled.
>
> 2 KINGS 7:5-7

Talk about an amplification system! The Syrians heard four leprous men walking down the desert in their sandals, and the Syrians thought it was a great army with chariots, horses, and sounds of armies marching. When they heard it, they took off running. They were so scared that they left everything behind at the camp.

Notice the time that this happened. It says in verse 7 that they fled at twilight: the exact time the four lepers got up and headed for their camp. Results came when the lepers decided to quit sitting there watching the situation happen and got up to do something about it. They did something different. They stepped out of their comfort zone and took a chance, and as they got up and stepped out, God moved in on their behalf.

Often we want to wait for God to do something. When we're under attack, we can move into a spiritual shock mode. When bombs are blowing up, you tend to hang limp. You are there, but that's it. Get up and move.

People often take Isaiah 40:31 out of context. It says, "Those who wait on the Lord shall renew their strength." Many read the wait part of this verse and think it means to do nothing. They become stuck there and believe it is spiritual to do nothing. "I'm waiting on God," they will say. "Just waiting for God to do something."

They miss the part in this same verse about how "they shall mount up with wings like eagles, they shall run and not be weary, they shall walk and not faint" (Isa. 40:31). Someone who mounts up like an eagle is not just sitting there doing nothing. Running and walking take action. And then there's verse 29, which says, "He gives power to the weak, and to those who have no might He increases strength." God wouldn't give us power, might, and strength if He only wanted us to wait.

So, the ball is in your court. The Bible says that when you draw near to God, God draws near to you. (James 4:8.) You take one step; God takes two. God is the One waiting for you to get up and do something. The second you get up to move toward your destiny—*swoosh!* He is right there to move on your behalf.

The word *wait* in Isaiah 40:31 actually means "to bind together by twisting, to look at with ardent expectation." That is moving forward and pressing in.

God wants us to rise up and be the men and women He's called us to be. We need to think like the four leprous men did. "Why sit we here 'til we die?" they said. "Let's get up and go!" (2 Kings 7:3,4.)

> When these lepers came to the outskirts of the camp, they went into one tent and ate and drank, and carried from it silver and gold and clothing, and went and hid them; then they came back and entered another tent, and carried some from there also, and went and hid it.
>
> 2 KINGS 7:8

They realized the first two tents were only the beginning. They looked around at the empty camp and saw thousands upon thousands of dwelling places, full of silver, gold, clothing, and food. After they finished chowing down and hiding the things from the first tents, they went to tell the others in Samaria. We need to let the people know that there's a whole heap of munchies here for a feast!

They go tell the king's household, and the king sends his servants to check it out. When they find out that it's true, all the people rush off to plunder the tents. Everyone in the city was blessed—except for that one man mentioned in verse two who openly doubted the word of the Lord from Elisha.

When Elisha prophesied that "tomorrow about this time a seah of fine flour shall be sold for a shekel, and two seahs of barley for a shekel, at the gate of Samaria" (2 Kings 7:1), this officer said, "Yeah, right! Even if God were to throw open the floodgates of heaven, I don't believe this could ever happen!" Well, after he said that, Elisha told him, "In fact, you shall see it with your eyes, but you shall not eat of it" (v. 2). And, sure enough, when everyone rushed out to get and sell the goodies the next day, just as the Lord had prophesied, he got trampled to death. He saw it and heard it but missed out because of doubt and unbelief.

Doubt and unbelief can keep us from the blessings God has for us. Faith moves the hand of God. Hebrews 11:6 says that "without faith it is impossible to please Him." No matter how bad your situation seems, remember what God did in Samaria. Remember all the promises of God. God turned the situation in Samaria around in twenty-four hours. He can do the same for you, but you must be willing to get up and do something. If you want to see God's hand move on your behalf, you need to do your part.

I am not talking about a struggle in the flesh. Don't run off and try to do things in your own strength. Rise up out of your depression and despair and move into the plan of God, resting in His strength. Get up out of complacency and give God something to work with.

A young lady came up to me after one of my services and said, "You know, Eastman, we had a real financial need. Some people owed us money and we really needed a major breakthrough. We had given and sown. We were praying and believing God for our finances, but things were rough. When we prayed, I felt that I needed to move and not just sit there. I picked up the phone and called the people who owed us money, and they said they could send us a check that same day." They received payment.

Give God Something To Work With

Sometimes we just have to set our hand to something. God says in Deuteronomy 28:8 that He'll "command the blessing on you in your storehouses and in all to which you set your hand." God cannot bless what you set your hand to unless you put your hand to it. Further along in verse 12 of this same chapter in Deuteronomy, God says that He will "bless all the work of your hand." He did not say, "I'll bless your hands even if they're just lying around doing nothing for Me."

The Bible tells the story of the prophet Samuel anointing Saul as king of Israel. Saul had disobeyed God, and Samuel's heart was grieved for Israel. He wanted them to serve the Lord more than anything, but it was not happening. He went to the altar and cried out to God to touch his nation and King Saul. God responded in 1 Samuel 16:1: "How long will you mourn for Saul, seeing I have rejected him from reigning over Israel? Fill your horn with oil, and go." He told Samuel to quit crying about the situation, get up, and do something about it.

Self-pity will keep you from advancement. I refuse to tolerate self-pity in my life. I made this decision while I was traveling. I was going to preach in a little church, and I prayed, "Lord, why is it so hard? Why is it so tough to preach here?" God gave me a picture of what self-pity looks like. I saw a little man who looked to be about 150 years old. He was bowed over, gnarled up, and had dirt clods on his head. His flesh was falling off, his breath was foul, his teeth were rotting out of his head, his clothes were stinky, and he had mucous coming out of his eyes. He was nasty.

Then God showed me how Self-Pity operates. He looks up at people and says, *It's so baaaadd.* He breathes all that horrible breath on them. They look down at him and say, "It is bad." In his evil voice he says, *No one understands what you're going through. Haaaaa.* And he breathes on them. They look down at him and say, "But you understand," and they pick him up and embrace him. They love him, kiss him, and take him to breakfast, and all the while their face is downcast because they keep looking down at this ugly little guy. Then they take him to work and wonder, *Why is it that when I walk into a room, people flee?*

Mr. Stinky is all over you. You stink because Self-Pity is right there with you. Everywhere you go, he goes. You bring him home. You bring him to bed with you. You bring him into your marriage and relationships.

When he first comes to you, he tells you he is your friend. But look out! He desires to devastate you. You need to kick Self-Pity out of the house. He is your enemy, and an ugly, stinky one!

Self-pity is a tactic of the enemy to get us off our path of destiny. "Oh, why does all this stuff keep happening to me? Why can't I ever get ahead? The world is just against me. Everyone hates me. Nothing is working for me. I guess I'm just destined to fail." Quit that! You are talking yourself right out of your true destiny! Kick that ugly old Self-Pity out of your mind and your mouth! Pick up your feet and get as far away from him as fast as you can.

> Strengthen the hands which hang down, and the feeble knees, and make straight paths for your feet, so that what is lame may not be dislocated, but rather be healed.
>
> HEBREWS 12:12,13

Paul and Silas had a wonderful opportunity for self-pity when they were thrown into prison. They were doing what God called them to do. They went to Philippi, preached, cast the devil out of a person, and were thrown into jail. Now, if that's not a good opportunity to start whining to God, I don't know what is! They could have cried, "Oh, God! All we want to do is serve You, but now look at us. We were whipped and our backs are bleeding. We are stuck in this prison with our feet in stocks. Oh, God!" They could have sung, "Nobody knows the trouble I've seen...." But that's not the song they sang.

The Bible says in Acts 16:25-26 that they began to sing praises to God, and as they were praising God, an earthquake opened the prison doors and they were free.

The devil wants to take advantage of you using self-pity. Refuse to be a target for the devil. Stand up and kick the devil out of your way! Rise in faith and walk right over the top of the enemy to get to your destiny! Don't just sit there. Get up, release your faith, and do something.

Reasons vs. Excuses

There's a big difference between a reason for doing something and an excuse for doing something (or not doing something). When you make excuses for yourself, you allow yourself to stagnate. You can sit there until you die. Quit making excuses and identify the problem, and then REPENT! Repentance produces change.

When a problem is identified as sin, it leads to repentance. It washes you in the blood of Jesus, and you are free to go on. The Bible tells us that the blood of Jesus Christ cleanses us from all sin. It does not say that it cleanses us from excuses. First John 1:9 says, "If we confess our sin, God is faithful and just to forgive us our sin." We'll go a lot further in life when we are quick to repent rather than make excuses.

Once while I was preaching in a church, a lady in a wheelchair came forward for prayer. My heart went out to her, and I knew in my heart that God was going to do something big in her life. As I approached her, I asked, "Ma'am, what is it you need?"

"I just want strength," she told me. "I was in a car wreck several years ago, and I've been paralyzed and unable to walk since that car accident. I'm just praying for strength."

So I am thinking, *Okay, praise God! Strength! Strength will flow through her body. Strength to get up, walk, run, leap, and shout!* So I put my Holy Spirit hands on her and began to command the nerves to line up with the Word of God and the power of God to flow through her body. Suddenly she stopped me and said, "Sir, I wish you wouldn't pray like that."

"Why? What's wrong?" I asked.

"Please don't pray like that," she repeated.

"Why?" I asked her.

"Because God has taught me so much. He gave me this accident and caused me to be paralyzed, and, well, He has done so much for me. I don't want to have to start all over again."

I just looked at her. "What?"

"God did this to me," she said.

As I looked at her, I felt righteous indignation rise inside of me. I thought of religious lies that had tried to slap sickness and disease on people and tell them sickness is the cross God has called them to bear.

I could have taken the Word of God and beat her with it. I wanted to tell her, "God didn't do that to you, ma'am. The Word says—*Wha-pam! Wha-pam!*" Many Scriptures talk about how God wants to heal and deliver us, and how it's not God who puts sickness or accidents or paralysis on us.

Rather than slam her with the truth, I met her where she was. "Ma'am," I said, "there was a time in my life when I probably would've leaned toward what you're talking about. But the more I know God and study His Word, the more I realize the truth." Then I explained to her how we do not want to blame God for something the devil has done. I shared Scriptures with her, like John 10:10, where Jesus said He came to give us life and to give it to us more abundantly. "Paralysis isn't abundant life. God has something so much better for you than that. God wants to flow through you. Ma'am, I know this is a lot, but would you let me lay hands on you and just pray for you and allow the Holy Spirit to be real to you?"

"Okay," she said.

So I prayed with her, and then I said, "Now you just sit here and worship God and let Him touch you."

I went back up to the platform, and while the congregation was worshiping God, I heard a big commotion. It sounded like a football game. A big roaring sound swept over the whole congregation. I turned to see what was going on, and the woman I had prayed with had gotten out of her wheelchair and was walking. She was still a little wobbly, but she was up and walking! Praise God! She had decided, "Why sit here 'til I die? No. I'm getting up!" She got up, and God gave her a miracle!

Don't Wait 'Til You Feel Like It

There are times when you roll out of bed in the morning that you don't feel like going to work. You do not feel like doing what you know you are supposed to be doing. But sometimes you've got to flat out put one foot in front of the other and just do it.

I remember one time when I was getting ready for one of our crusades, and I was sick and tired. I didn't feel well, my stomach hurt, and I had a fever. But I had given my word that I was going to preach at this crusade, and I was determined to do it.

My wife helped me pack, and I crawled to the car, got in, tipped the seat back, and put my hands up to worship God as my wife drove me to the airport. "Oh, Father," I prayed, "thank You that Your healing power flows through me."

When we got to the airport, my wife got my suitcase out of the trunk for me, handed it to me, and said, "Honey, go give them heaven." I was thinking, *Aw, come on. Couldn't you give me some sympathy here? At least ask me if I'd like to stay home.* But no. "Go give 'em heaven! I know you're as sick as a dog, but (swift kick) get out there and give it to them, honey."

My wife knows about faithfulness. She knew that I had promised to preach. She knew that God would honor my faithfulness with His own faithfulness. She was not about to encourage me to stay home.

While the airplane was taking off, the healing power of God hit me. *Bam!* I was healed—right there on American Airlines!

But I could have missed it if I had given in to my feelings. I could have just stayed home and whimpered and moaned instead of getting up and doing what I knew God had called me to do. I kept heading in the direction of my destiny because I am determined to live by God's Word, not my feelings.

The time to make a decision to fulfill your dream is not when you wake up in the morning and say, "Well, I'll see if I feel like it or not." If you wait for a feeling, you will never get to what God has called you to do. You have to decide to make it happen. Don't just stick your toe in the water and see if you like the temperature or not. Make a decision to jump in and stick with it. You can complete what God has called you to do. When you are faithful in the small things, God will make you ruler over much. (Matt. 25:21,23.)

You don't feel your way into action. You act your way into feeling. People often think feelings will motivate them to get up and do what they are called to do. Feelings can change from moment to moment. They are not constant, and if you follow your feelings, you will go up and down just as they do.

You have to do it. It is up to you. God is there to give you all the power and provision you need to get there, but you must fulfill your dream for yourself. That is your part.

Don't Wait Until Everything Is Perfect

I have heard people say, "I'll just wait 'til after I get out of college before I start heading toward my dreams," or "I'll wait 'til the money comes in." They end up waiting and waiting and never find the perfect opportunity to start toward their destiny.

The Word of God reminds us that "he who observes the wind [and waits for all conditions to be favorable] will not sow, and he who regards the clouds will not reap" (Eccl. 11:4 AMP). Your time is now. You are in the right place. God created you for such a time as this. Make a decision to move in the direction you know God is calling you to fulfill the dream He has given you.

I have noticed that every time we have ever taken a step in ministry or in business, the money has never come before we take that step. As we have stepped out in faith, God has always provided the money. As we discussed in Chapter Two, first, you have to have a vision. Once you have the vision, move forward. As you move toward the vision God has put in your heart, you will see the provision come. First the vision comes, then you take the steps and provision comes.

One day my wife and I were having dinner with a friend of ours, Mark Brazee. He began to tell me about the revival and the hunger of the people, and how God was moving in those nations. Mark has ministered in the former communist bloc countries and works a great deal in Europe. I asked him, "How's everything going?"

He said, "I don't know of twenty churches in all of Europe that I can really recommend for people to go to."

"Why?" I asked.

"Because people aren't planting churches. They are just sitting there. The churches that are there are okay, but they're not developing because new churches are not being planted."

"Why is that?" I wanted to know.

"Because socialism has taken the pioneer spirit out of people. Unless someone stands over them and gives them provision for the next step, they generally will not do anything. They will not do anything before they get the building, the chairs, the sound system, the ushers, the greeters, and everything they need first. Only then will they start doing it."

That is how many Christians are. It's not just in Europe. We wait for the government to tell us we can do it. We wait for this person or that one to take the first step. Quit that! Don't just sit there! Do something!

When I was in Bible college, I didn't wait until after I graduated to start preaching. I didn't wait until I had that little certificate that said "Now You Can Go Preach." I went on the weekends and ministered in little churches. Sometimes, if I did not have an invitation, I would invite myself. I would knock on doors and say, "Hi, I'm Eastman Curtis. I've got some good news for you and it will change your life." I would tell people about Jesus. I would walk into nursing homes and say, "Hi, I'm here to minister." We wheeled out people in their wheelchairs and I preached to them.

I was not going to wait for an invitation. I took steps right then to fulfill what God had placed in my heart.

I like what it says in Ecclesiastes 9:10 in the New American Standard Version: "Whatever your hand finds to do, verily, do it with all your might." Give it everything you have. Do not be satisfied with just a little. It may not be done perfectly, but so what! God is not asking you to be perfect. He is asking you to get up and do something with Him. He is asking you to set your hand to the plow and do what He has placed in your heart to do. Don't let anything rob you of the pioneer spirit. "And whatever you do, do it heartily, as to the Lord" (Col. 3:23).

Don't just sit there—do something!

Chapter 7

Destiny Requires Miracles

Fulfilling your dream requires the supernatural power of God, including miracles.

Jesus was anointed with the Holy Spirit and with power. Acts 10:38 tells us "how God anointed Jesus of Nazareth with the Holy Spirit and with power, who went about doing good and healing all who were oppressed by the devil, for God was with Him."

Jesus is our example, our role model. If we want to accomplish great things for God, we are going to need the Holy Spirit and power from on high. Jesus told His disciples that He would send the Holy Spirit to them after He returned to heaven. "Behold, I send the Promise of My Father upon you; but tarry in the city of Jerusalem until you are endued with power from on high" (Luke 24:49). In addition, in Acts 1:8 Jesus says, "You shall receive power when the Holy Spirit has come upon you." Our power to do miracles comes from the power of the Holy Spirit in us. It is the power of God working in and through us.

When the Holy Spirit came upon the disciples as recorded in Acts 2, they began to preach as never before. When Peter stood up to preach after having received the Holy Spirit, three thousand people listening to him were saved on the spot. When the Spirit-filled disciples began to lay hands on sick or demonized people, those people were miraculously healed and delivered from the bondage of Satan.

Before they received power from the Holy Spirit, the very same disciples struggled with what Jesus told them and tried to teach them. The disciples ran off in fear when Jesus was taken away to be crucified, but when they were filled with the Holy Spirit at Pentecost, things changed. They changed. They were suddenly filled with the power of God. They were "endued with power from on high" (Luke 24:49). That made all the difference. We cannot do mighty works of God without the Holy Spirit. If we are to advance in our destiny and accomplish our dream, we must do so with the power of God.

Going Beyond Your Own Abilities

Abide in Me, and I in you. As the branch cannot bear fruit of itself, unless it abides in the vine, neither can you, unless you abide in Me. I am the vine, you are the branches. He who abides in Me, and I in him, bears much fruit; for without Me you can do nothing.

If you abide in Me, and My words abide in you, you will ask what you desire, and it shall be done for you.

JOHN 15:4,5,7

When God gives you a dream, it will require you to go beyond your own natural abilities. His purpose and plan for you will go beyond your education, natural skills, or anything you could accomplish on your own. God desires for you to operate in His anointing and His power rather than your own limitations. God has a plan for you that will amaze you when you tap into it, but it requires supernatural miracles from God to accomplish it.

When I was first born again, I tried to do much in my own strength. I had two categories: the things I could do by myself, and the things I needed God to help me with. I would think, *Well, I can do this okay. I know how to do this. But this thing over here, that is a big one. That is going to take a miracle. So I need Your help on this, God.* I would invite the presence of God to move into only certain parts of my life.

As I continue to grow closer to God, I have discovered I need God in every part of my life—even things that I thought I could do by myself. I realize I experience a much better result when God has His sleeves rolled up and is involved with me. I am not in this thing by myself. I am a co-laborer with Him in my life.

Mark 16:20 KJV says, "And they went forth, and preached everywhere, the Lord working with them, and confirming the word with signs following." God wants to work with us.

Do you need some signs and wonders in your finances, business, or family? God will never intrude, so you must invite Him into these areas of your life. God is able, but you have to ask Him to work in your life. You cannot do it by yourself.

My grandma used to say, "If you ever see a turtle on a fence post, I can guarantee someone put that turtle up there." No one ever says, "Wow, look at that leaping turtle! That's one climbing turtle." That turtle did not leap up on that fence post. Someone put him there.

We are who we are because of the grace of God. We have done what we have done because of the grace of God.

In John 15:5 Jesus tells us that when we abide in Him and His Word abides in us, we will bear "much fruit." That sounds like more than just getting your needs met. God wants to take us beyond barely enough. The Word says that if we delight ourselves in the Lord, He will give us the desires of our heart. (Ps. 37:4.)

As we discussed in Chapter Two, God wants you to have an abundant life. He tells us in John 10:10 that that is why He came: "I have come that [you] may have life, and that [you] may have it more abundantly." God wants you to have a surplus in order to be a blessing to other people. He wants you to bear much fruit for Him as you fulfill your destiny.

I want you to notice what Jesus says right after He tells us to bear much fruit: "Without Me you can do nothing" (John 15:5). We cannot do it without Him. I have found out that I have to stay dependent upon God in order to succeed in my calling. The closer I get to Him, the more I realize how much I need Him.

Paul reprimanded the Galatians for relying too much on their own abilities. "Having begun in the Spirit, are you now being made perfect by the flesh.... He who supplies the Spirit to you and works miracles among you, does He do it by the works of the law, or by the hearing of faith?" (Gal. 3:3,5).

There is a miraculous part of our destiny that we need to tap into. Sure, you can do some things in your own ability, but God wants you to supersede that. He wants you to move into the miraculous. It is going to take miracles to move in your destiny.

It's Going To Take Miracles

It took a miracle for the children of Israel to move out of the captivity of Egypt. It took a miracle for Moses to lift up his staff for the Red Sea to part. It took a miracle for the walls of Jericho to fall down so the people of God could move into their promises. It took a miracle for little David to slay Goliath. It took a miracle for him to get past obstacles to fulfill his destiny. It took a miracle for Jesus to turn water into wine and for Him to feed five thousand people with five loaves of bread and two fish. It took a miracle for an illiterate plumber by the name of Smith Wigglesworth literally to change a nation for the Gospel of Jesus Christ. It took a miracle for a little ex-burnout, beanbag-chair-sitting, lava-lamp-watching heathen like I was to see 52,000 people become born again last year in this ministry. It took a miracle to build a 2000-seat auditorium in a church that was not even two years old yet.

If we are going to move into what God has for us, it will take miracles. We are what we are by the grace of God. If we start saying, "Well, look at what I've done," we are moving into dangerous territory. When we start taking credit for what God has done, we stop growing in the arenas and avenues God has for us. I never want to stop growing and progressing in what God has for me.

In fact, we are setting goals and five-year plans. We are dreaming bigger dreams. The Spirit of God has really been dealing with me to stretch further and to go farther than I have ever gone before. We have seen Him do some great things, but we cannot camp there. We have to keep moving.

You don't want to get ahead of God, and you do not want to do more than you can handle, but that's not the problem for most people. Most people never do all that God has for them. God wants you to tap into His ability, His thinking, His talking, His walking, His power, and His manifestations and see great things take place.

Paul says in 1 Corinthians 2:4 KJV, "My speech and my preaching was not with enticing words of man's wisdom, but in demonstration of the Spirit and of power." Paul knew that everything he did for God went beyond his own abilities. He knew that he needed the power of the Holy Spirit to accomplish his destiny. Paul had some natural abilities. He was well-educated, trained in the best institutions, and an intelligent man, but it was not until he tapped into the miracle power of God that he was able to accomplish the ministry God gave him.

He had done many things in his own abilities before he received the Lord. God stopped him in his tracks and gave him a taste of the power of God, and Paul was never the same after that.

Sure, we can do some things with human wisdom, but there's so much more God wants to do, so much more than we could ever even dream of doing on our own.

One time when Angel and I were preaching in Charlotte, North Carolina, some people brought a lady to be prayed for. They lifted her out of her wheelchair and helped her walk to the front. I could see she was very weak. She told me the doctors had given up on her and had given her two weeks to live.

When I prayed for her, I could feel the power of God flowing through her. I don't always feel something when I pray for people. I have seen people healed either way. I know it is not dependent on what we feel, but this time I could tell God was doing a miracle. She lifted her hands and rejoiced in her healing. She went back to her wheelchair, but I could see she was excited.

When we went back there seven months later, I saw her in the front row. She was ecstatic. During worship, she got up and danced around, just worshiping God. At the end of the service, I asked her what had happened.

"Oh, honey," she said, "I have to tell you the miracle." She went back to the doctor after I prayed for her and told him to check her out because she was convinced that Jesus had healed her. The doctor said, "I appreciate your zeal, but I'm a cancer specialist so, trust me. You need to get your house in order."

She insisted that he check her out. He argued with her over it and said her insurance would not cover it, but she said she would pay for it herself. When they ran the tests, the doctor could not find one trace of cancer in her body. She was healed by the power of God.

Thank God for people with gifts and talents and expertise. We need to use the natural abilities God gives us. But if that is where you stop, you can only get so far. If you lean on men's wisdom alone, it's going to limit what God will do in your life.

My wife and I were ministering at a church in Alabama. In the middle of my message, a young lady stood up and began to scream. That will get your attention. We stopped the service and asked her what was happening.

"As you were speaking," she said, "the most incredible thing happened." She told me how several years before she had punctured her cornea. "I haven't been able to see out of my eye since," she explained. "As you were talking about the power of God, I could suddenly see out of my eye! God healed my eye!"

God had just performed a miracle in her life while I was preaching. It was not a result of my persuasive words or fantastic preaching. It was a demonstration of the power of God. "My speech and my preaching was not with enticing words of man's wisdom, but in demonstration of the Spirit and of power: that your faith should not stand in the wisdom of men, but in the power of God" (1 Cor. 2:4,5 KJV).

Dare To Believe God for a Miracle

Sometimes I look back and think, *Wow! Five years ago I do not know that I even had the guts to dream what's taking place right now.* Sometimes it is hard for us to imagine what God will do in our lives. God wants to do things in your life that will go beyond your wildest dreams. You may think it cannot be done, but nothing is too hard for God. God's part is to perform the miracles. Your part is to believe He will perform them.

It can happen for you. Take what you have and use it to the glory of God. If all you have is a staff like Moses had, use it for God, and He will bring a miracle out of it. God is looking for someone who will dare to dream big. He is looking for someone who is willing to believe that He can do anything. He is looking for someone who will dare to believe that He has a miracle for them.

God created us to have fellowship with Him. He fashioned us to work together, to rule and reign with Him, for the sake of the kingdom. He wants us to be involved in kingdom business. We need Him, but He needs us too. That is why He told us we can do all things through Christ Jesus who strengthens us. (Phil. 4:13.)

On your own, there are many things you will not be able to do. But with God, anything is possible. We need to stay dependent on God. If you run off and try to do your own thing without Him, you won't get very far. You may think you are going somewhere for a while, but it will not take long for you to realize that you are limiting yourself. You can do way more when you work together with God. Remember, "with men this is impossible, but with God all things are possible" (Matt. 19:26).

As a child of God and a joint heir with Jesus, everything that belongs to God also belongs to you. Galatians 4:7 tells us that we are "no longer a slave but a son, and if a son, then an heir of God through Christ." You have access to everything of His: His miracle power, His abilities, His dreams for your life. All of it belongs to you. It is up to you to grab hold of it and use it. God will not make you take it. You have to reach out in faith and take hold of whatever miracle you need.

Hunger for the Miraculous

There is a yearning inside every person for miracles. Just look around you at all the programs on TV and in kids' games. My generation was brought up with all kinds of superheroes: Superman, Batman, Aquaman, and Wonder Woman. Some Christians say, "Oh, that stuff is all so bad. That's the world."

The world is searching for the supernatural. The devil takes advantage of that all right, but I believe it is going to backfire on the devil. God has a way of turning things around for His good. People are going to run to God when they discover that He is the real Superhero. People are tired of the fake, the phony, and the artificial miracles. When they see the real miracle power of God, nothing will be able to keep people back!

Within every person—whether a believer or non-believer—there is a God-given desire for miracles. Every one of us has been created in the image of God in order to have fellowship with God. Fellowship with God requires us to step into the realm of the supernatural, because God is a supernatural God. Even those who do not yet know God personally are instinctively drawn to the supernatural.

I experienced something that really impacted me regarding the hunger for miracles. I was preaching in Austin, Texas, at a youth convention. During one of the services, I saw a young man who had a Mohawk haircut. His hair must have stood up two feet tall. I do not know what kind of hair spray he used, but it had to be industrial strength. He had the colors of the rainbow painted all the way down the sides of it, his head was shaved on the sides, and there were big, pointed spikes coming off the top of his head. He looked like a porcupine.

I saw him while I was trying to preach. He was seated in the second row, and my eyes gravitated to him. He was hard to miss. He sat with his arms folded and wearing a vest without a shirt. He had one big hoop earring, which was no big deal. I had seen that before. He also had a nose ring. I had seen that before, too. But then I noticed something I had never seen before. I have seen it since then, but at that time, I had not seen anything like it. He had an earring in his nipple. Ouch! I remember thinking, *Ooh! That had to hurt.*

A gold chain ran from his ear to his nose, and then from his nose to his nipple. Well, I looked at that and I could just picture him having it done. "Okay, now you may feel a little pressure." *ZZzzzzyyowwrrr.* Whoa!

Remember all this is happening while I am trying to preach, but my imagination is doing some funny things. I envisioned someone coming up after the service with a fuzzy Angora sweater, and, when they give him a hug to welcome him, that chain gets stuck inside their sweater, and *swoosh—ahhhhhhhh!* I was picturing all this while I was trying to preach, but it gets even worse than that. I envisioned him driving his bicycle down the road when he comes upon an unassuming branch hanging down that catches on this chain and *Shhwwoopp!* He is swept up off his bike. There he is just hanging from the branch by this chain. *Yowwrrhhh!*

I was trying to bring every thought into the captivity of Christ, and it was a miracle that I made it through that service! When I finished preaching, I gave an altar call. I glanced over at him, but he just sat there, not budging. I dared God to move on him. I did notice, however, that the young lady beside him was receiving from God.

I gave a call for the baptism in the Holy Spirit, and many people came forward to be filled with the Spirit. I invited anyone who needed healing to lay hands on themselves to receive from God. We did a mass prayer like this because there were too many for me to lay hands on and pray for individually. (There were several thousand people there.) Then, after a time of worship, I encouraged everyone who had received an instant miracle to come on up to the front and testify.

When the young lady sitting beside this man with the chain in his nipple came up, she began to tell how she had worn glasses all her life and was never able to read without corrective lenses. "But God just healed my eyes," she said. "I don't need my glasses anymore!" She wore thick glasses that she had taken off. I opened my Bible and let her read from it, and she started reading the Word of God without her glasses. We were all rejoicing!

I noticed that while she was testifying the young man with the Mohawk stood up and watched. He began to cry. Mascara ran down his cheeks. There he was, big Mohawk and earrings, just standing there sobbing.

As we closed the service, he came up to me and said, "I want to tell you something. I don't know about all this other stuff, and I don't know these other people, but that girl with the eyes—I know her. We grew up in church together." He said his dad was a deacon and he had been running from God all his life. "My mom made me come to this thing," he told me. "I didn't want to come here. I know that girl. I know what her eyes were like. I used to steal her glasses when I was five years old, and we would make fun of her because she would run into people and bump into walls. That was a miracle." Then he said, "If God would just be real to me, I'd serve Him with all my heart."

I figured when anyone who pierces their nipple says they will do something with all their heart, they will do it. It takes serious commitment to pierce a nipple. Besides, I had seen him cry and I saw his passion. I heard his heart cry. I started laughing. "Buddy," I told him, "you get ready. God is going to show Himself real because you want Him to and He is real. You lift your hands up in the air and get ready."

He put his hands up, and before I could even get my hands on him, God got to him. I walked up to him and *boom!* He fell out under the power of God. The cool thing was that he did not even need anyone to catch him because of that Mohawk which kept his head about a foot off the ground. That thing cushioned the blow. So there he was on the floor just crying and worshiping God and speaking in other tongues. The power of God was all over him. He was literally vibrating under the presence of God.

This young man's youth group ran over to him and started taking pictures. "This is incredible," they were sobbing. "You don't know this guy. This is incredible!" All the while he lay on the floor worshiping God.

This generation is screaming for the power of God. This nation is crying for signs and wonders. Now is not the time to back off. Now is not the time to limit our dreams and our goals. It is time to dream dreams and pray prayers like never before.

Now is the time for miracles! If we are going to fulfill our destiny, it is going to take the miracle power of Almighty God.

Seek the Miracle-Worker

God wants a relationship with us. He wants to get our attention. He loves us so much and longs to have fellowship with us. Miracles help us notice Him. They make us aware that He is real after all. Sometimes people become so focused on the miracles themselves that they forget about the Miracle-Worker. As wonderful as miracles are, God is more wonderful than all of them put together. It's so important to remember this and to keep our hearts where they belong.

I once heard a story about a group called Chataqua speakers. They were professional orators back in the 1800s who traveled around the country telling stories and reciting poetry. They gathered in huge auditoriums and spoke in front of all who came to hear them. People were so impressed with how well they handled the English language. This was before radio and television, so people loved to listen to Chataqua speakers paint beautiful pictures with words. They spent much time practicing how to articulate their words. They practiced voice inflections and increased their vocabulary so they could perfect their speech.

One particular Chataqua speaker always closed his speech with the Twenty-third Psalm. He knew right where to put the voice inflections, and, at the end of it, people would applaud.

At the end of one of his meetings, an old man from the audience got out of his seat and made his way up to the front. He went up to this Chataqua speaker and said, "Sir, would you mind if I quoted the Twenty-third Psalm?" Well, this man looked like he had seen better days. You could hardly hear him. His voice sounded like it had been all blown out.

The Chataqua speaker just smiled and said, "Well, if you want to do it after this, it's just going to make me look that much better." But the old man still wanted to do it. "Go on up and help yourself," the Chataqua speaker told him.

This old man stood behind the platform and began to quote the Twenty-third Psalm in this raspy voice. "The Lord is my Shepherd. I shall not want." Suddenly, it got quiet as he continued reciting this Scripture with all eyes on him. The people began to weep, and when this old man stepped off, the crowd stood to their feet and gave him such a thunderous ovation that it blew the Chataqua speaker away. He had never heard anything like it before.

Here he had practiced all these years and was professionally trained, and then this raspy old retired preacher gets up and takes the whole audience with him. He looked at all the people, then he looked at the elderly man and could not understand why he had been able to carry this out so powerfully. He grabbed the old man by the arm. "I don't understand this," he said. "I've gone to school for this. I have practiced. I have rehearsed. I have the right voice inflections. Yet I have never seen words move a crowd like your words have done. I've quoted the Twenty-third Psalm for years, but I've never seen this type of response."

"Young man," the old retired preacher told him. "You know the Twenty-third Psalm but I know the Author of the Twenty-third Psalm. That's what makes the difference."

I don't want to just know about miracles. I want to know the Miracle-Worker. God wants to give you miracles, but more than anything else, He longs to walk with you and talk with you. He wants a relationship with you. He longs to pour His dreams and goals into your heart and take you beyond your wildest imaginations. It starts with delighting in Him and seeking Him with all your heart. Then He will give you all the desires of your heart.

There is only one thing that will fill the void in all of us, and that is an intimate relationship with Jesus Christ. Seek first the kingdom of God and His righteousness, and all these other things will be added to you. (Matt. 6:33.) God wants to bless you more than you can even imagine. He wants you to obtain more than you can dream up because He loves you. You are the apple of His eye. He longs to talk with you and share everything with you. He longs for you to run up to Him with a great big hug and tell Him how much He means to you.

As a father, I know how much it means when my kids do this to me. I just love it when my kids crawl up on my lap and wrap their arms around my neck and start talking to me. I love it when we spend time together. It's great when we do fun things together, but I love when we just hang out, too. If I'm like that with my earthly kids, how much more is our heavenly Father like that with us?

When God does exciting things for us, we can become caught up in the great things. It is wonderful when God does great things for us, but it is greater still to be caught up with Him. When that priority is out of line, everything under that priority will be out of line.

God has great things in store for you, and it is going to take the miraculous. It will also take a relationship with him to see your dream happen.

Chapter 8

Destiny Requires Focus

In Acts 26, Paul is talking to King Agrippa after his arrest by the Jews for preaching Christ. He was brought before the king to be tried in court and was given the opportunity to speak in his own defense. After explaining some of his background to the king, Paul told him what happened to him on the way to Damascus. He explained how a bright light from heaven arrested him and how the Lord Jesus spoke to him.

He testified before the whole court of Jesus' words to him regarding his mandate from God. "Rise and stand on your feet; for I have appeared to you *for this purpose*" (Acts 26:16). I have italicized the words "for this purpose" here because I want you to see that God didn't give Paul a whole long list of things to focus on in his ministry. He gave him one specific purpose.

I really believe that when God gives you a destiny, He gives you one particular thing to focus on. This is just a personal conviction, but I really believe that God gives every one of us a specific message. For some, it may be a message of restoration. For others, it may be a message of joy. I believe that we all have one thing—one dream, one message—that flows through our veins. If someone were to squeeze you up against a wall, that is what will come out.

There may be some people who have more than one vision. However, even if God does give someone twin visions, they will complement each other. They need to be compatible or harmonious. In other words, they should not be pulling that person in opposite directions. If they are, then at least one of the visions cannot be from God, because God will not split someone in two different directions.

Jesus told us that a house divided against itself could not stand. (Luke 11:17.) God may be into multiplication, but He is not into division. If you feel that you have more than one vision in your heart, seek the Lord in prayer and find out which one—if any—is really the one thing you are to focus on.

How often do you get in a car and start driving without having any idea where you are going? Now, granted, sometimes we will go for a drive to think about something, to relax, or to pray. However, most of us know where we are headed when we get in a car and start driving. We have a goal in mind. We are going to work, or we're going to the store, or we're taking the kids to school. We don't usually drive around aimlessly; we have a destination in mind, and so we head in that direction. That is what God wants us to do when He gives us a destiny to move into.

Many people run around with no idea what they are really supposed to be doing, and often that is why they are unhappy. When you know what your purpose in life is, it gives you something to live for. Without a sense of direction, you are depressed and frustrated. You can become involved in the wrong things. You snap at people and grumble. When you know exactly what you are supposed to do, it does something inside you. As you begin moving toward something specific, it charges you up. You have to get to where you are going.

Paul knew exactly what God had called him to do. In Acts 26:18, Paul gives us his mission statement: To open the eyes of the Gentiles, to turn them from darkness to light, and from the power of Satan to God, that they may receive forgiveness of sins and an inheritance among those who are sanctified by faith in God. This was the purpose burning in Paul's heart. It flowed out of his mouth. He ate, slept, and dreamed about it. It was his whole focus. "One thing I do," he said, "forgetting those things which are behind and reaching forward to those things which are ahead, I press toward the goal for the prize of the upward call of God in Christ Jesus" (Phil. 3:13,14).

Paul understood exactly what God had called him to do, and he did it. After he told King Agrippa what the Lord had told him to do, he said, "I was not disobedient to the heavenly vision" (Acts 26:19). He was faithful to do all that God called him to do because he did not become side-tracked. He stayed focused on the one thing God had called him to do and gave himself fully to it.

What if we all knew the reason why God had placed us here on this earth? And what if we were to focus on this one thing as Paul did? I believe we could change the world.

It is time to focus. If we would all focus on that one thing God has given each of us to accomplish, the devil would get so nervous that he would have to go out and buy Depends underwear. If each of us would apply our God-given talents and abilities to whatever purpose He has given us to fulfill, it would impact the whole world.

Your Purpose Should Permeate Your Whole Life

Once you discover what your one essential purpose is, it will show up in every part of who you are. It will come out through your lifestyle, actions, finances, words, and relationships. It will permeate every part of your life, because it is what keeps you motivated. Whatever your focus is on will dominate your life. If you focus on worldly things, that is the direction in which you will go. If you focus on the purpose God has for you, that is what you will accomplish.

You need to understand that the devil would love to get you sidetracked from your mission in order to keep you from your destiny. He wants you focused on anything but that one assignment you're supposed to accomplish on earth. He will try to get many Christians involved in substitute activities—all good things, but not the right things. They get busy with the good things in the name of "God" when these activities are not the things they should be doing at all. They may be good things, and they may even need to be done, but that doesn't mean that you are necessarily the one who should be doing them.

Many have the mentality that as long as they are doing something good, they are on the right track. The devil loves to keep Christians occupied with things that rob them of the time and energy needed to accomplish their God-given dream; things that keep them going through the motions while never really obtaining their full potential.

God wants you to be effective and desires you to succeed even more than you want to succeed. He is looking over your shoulder, rolling up His sleeves, eager to get involved in your dream. He is on your side, rooting for you. He wants you to get on track and stay on track.

Three Things That Keep You From Your Dream

There are several things that can keep you from doing what you are really supposed to be doing—things that will keep you from fulfilling your dream.

1. Fear

The first thing that we have to hit head on is fear. Many people are afraid of change, so they just keep doing what they have always done rather than trying something different. John 12:42 describes something that still happens with many people today: "Even among the rulers many believed in Him, but because of the Pharisees they did not confess Him, lest they should be put out of the synagogue; for they loved the praise of men more than the praise of God" (John 12:42,43). They were afraid that they would not be accepted. They were afraid of how people might react if they followed the will of God.

How many people do the very same thing today? How many of us worry more about what people will think of us than about accomplishing what God has given us to do? "They loved the praise of men more than the praise of God" (v. 42). Are you more concerned about pleasing people than God? What is your real motivation for volunteering in every possible church activity or community function available? Is it because God has really told you to do these things, or is it to impress people? Is it to impress the pastor, other Christians, or your friends? Why are you doing the things you are doing? Think about it. Why do you spend so much time polishing your car? Is it something God has called you to spend all your time on, or is it to impress others? What about all the time you spend fussing with your house? Does everything really need to be spotless and immaculate all the time? Do you really need to spend all your free time shopping for more home improvements and fancy decorations?

I am not saying you should just let everything go. Of course we have responsibilities. Where is your focus? Where are you investing most of your time and energy? If it is not doing that one thing God has called you to focus on, then you are sidetracked.

So many times we are caught up in our image. What will people think? What will they say about me? Will they think I am a slob if my house isn't perfect? What will they think if I say no when they ask me to help in the church? How can I not go on that outreach when everyone else is going? Will they think I am not a good Christian? We can get so preoccupied with what others may think about us that we never step into what God really has for us. The list goes on and on. So we just keep running in circles all based in fear: fear of rejection. God has more for you than that.

If you want to move forward in your destiny, you have to face fear head on. Rather than be concerned about what other people think about you, focus in on who you really are. Stop worrying about how you appear, and focus on your identity. Instead of trying to be what everyone else thinks you should be, be who God says you should be. Instead of doing everything to please everyone, focus on pleasing God.

It does not matter how people perceive you. What matters is who and what you are before God. When Jesus walked the face of the earth, He did not try to appear good. We all know He was good, but He did not have to prove it to anyone around Him, He knew who He was and what He was there to accomplish. He didn't try to give the appearance of healing. He was healing! He didn't have to run all over town trying to convince people that He was a prophet and a teacher. He knew who He was and what He was about. He just got on with it.

That is what we need to do. We need to just get on with doing the work God has called us to do and be who He has called us to be. Rather than get all caught up in the way that you appear, just be. Be what God has called you to be. It will set you free.

2. Doing Good Things vs. Your God Thing

Now in those days, when the number of the disciples was multiplying, there arose a complaint against the Hebrews by the Hellenists, because their widows were neglected in the daily distribution. Then the twelve summoned the multitude of the disciples and said, "It is not desirable that we should leave the word of God and serve tables. Therefore, brethren, seek out from among you seven men of good reputation, full of the Holy Spirit and wisdom, whom we may appoint over this business; but we will give ourselves continually to prayer and to the ministry of the word."

ACTS 6:1-4

What if Peter, John, and the early church leaders had sought to please the people and taken the time to serve tables? They would not have had the time to preach and teach the Word. They would have been bogged down with this job and would never have gotten around to what they were really called to do. Thank God, these men had the wisdom of God. They knew what they were supposed to be doing. They knew that they did not have time to feed the people and continue giving themselves fully to prayer and the ministry of the Word. They knew it would pull them off course from their calling.

Notice they did not neglect to meet the needs of the people. They saw to it that the problem was resolved. They began to delegate. They found others who were gifted to take care of this other business. We need to remember that God has given every one of us something particular to do in the body of Christ. When everyone does their part, things run smoothly.

Sometimes leaders think they need to do everything themselves or it won't be done right, and they short-circuit themselves by using up the time and energy meant to be invested in that one thing God has called them to focus on. Not only do they burn themselves out; they prevent someone else from stepping into that role he or she was created to fulfill.

We need to be careful not to get caught up in doing all kinds of good things that end up preventing us from getting to the God thing: that specific thing God has for us to do. If we want to be effective in our calling, we need to stay focused.

Many times pastors are sidetracked from their vision by being wrapped up in all kinds of projects in the church. Often these are good projects, but as pastors, they must determine what lines up with their vision and stick with that. The same is true for us; we cannot do everything. It is important to identify God's vision for your life and run with it. Sure, you will get people who will criticize you for not taking up their project. Who are you going to seek to please? Men or God? You decide.

I remember how, years ago, I used to run to the back of the church after I finished ministering the Word to run my own tape table. I thought it was humble of me to do everything myself. I found out it was not humble but dumb because, while I was at the back selling tapes, there would be people up at the front who needed prayer. The whole time I was back at the tape table, God had called someone else to be there selling those tapes. But there I was, holding someone else back from being a part of the ministry. They could have been excelling in their gifts and doing what God had called them to do, while I was busy doing what God had called me to do.

We are not meant to be a one-man show. It is about everyone working together, about the whole body of Christ flowing together as one, with each person doing his or her part to make it happen.

In life there can be so many interesting things to do. We are moving along in a certain direction when we see something else that grabs us. And we think, *Hey that would be nice, too. Yeah. That is a good idea. That sounds great.* Sure it is great. There are many great ideas out there. But if you try to do them all, you will end up gasping for air.

You are too wiped out to get on with the plan you should have been focusing on to begin with. When you try to do too many things at the same time, you can water down the desire God has put in your heart. When you aim for that one thing, you will see the blessings of God overtake you.

People can have what they think is a passion, but it is not their passion. They saw someone else do it, so they think that is what they should do. There are all kinds of good ideas out there. However, there are good ideas and God ideas. We need to do what God has called us to do, not what someone (or everyone) else says we should do.

I know someone who loves to tell everyone what he or she needs to do. If you do not have a plan for your life, he has a plan for you. When I sit down with this man, before three minutes are up he says, "I tell you what you need to do, Eastman, to really increase your ministry." He goes off like a machine gun. There you have it: God's plan for your life (according to him). The first few times I sat down with him, I thought, *Man, I've got to write that down. I've got to do this stuff.* He was so convincing. He said it with such passion, such fervor, but that was what was in his heart, not mine.

You can learn to walk away from people like this. If you don't, they can pull you off course. We need to pursue what God puts in our own heart, not someone else's.

Is Your Cart Too Full?

People fill their schedules with good things, but they may never get around to doing what's best. It is like when you go grocery shopping with your kids. The smartest thing to do is to keep the kids inside the basket, because if they get out of that basket, you will come home with stuff you never wanted. If you have ever been grocery shopping with your kids, you know what I am talking about. There have been times when I've gone to the store with Sumner and Nicole to get milk and eggs, and suddenly I find myself pushing a cart loaded up with items I never went in to buy.

How many times do we do this in our Christian walk? We push our cart in a certain direction, and someone else loads us up with extra items. Soon we cannot even see over the top of it. We do not know what direction we are going because we have too much in our baskets. Throw it all off and re-evaluate. Why am I doing what I am doing? What has God called me to do? Am I doing it just to be doing it? Is this something God has really given me to do?

Don't allow substitute activity to hold you back. Go for the dream. Go for the vision God has put in your heart.

> One thing is needful: and Mary hath chosen that good part, which shall not be taken away from her.
>
> LUKE 10:42 KJV

Jesus was talking to Martha here. Martha was great at keeping very busy with many things. Her sister, Mary, was different. She had her priorities straight. She knew that the most important thing was to listen to Jesus and soak up everything that He was teaching.

Jesus told Martha that Mary had chosen "that good part." She chose to give herself fully to His word rather than to become wrapped up in substitute activity. She wasn't spending all her time and energy flipping burgers and wiping tables. That is not to say you should never do this. That is not what Jesus was saying here.

Know your priority. Where are you investing the biggest part of your time and energy? Are you giving yourself fully to that one thing God has given you to do? Are you preoccupied with all kinds of busy things that take you further and further from your purpose? One thing is needful. Are you doing it?

Jesus is saying the same thing to us today. One thing is needful. Choose to focus on that one thing I've given you to do. What is that "good part" God has given you to fulfill? Find that one thing you are destined to do, then do it with all your heart. Focus. Focus. Focus.

3. Being Busy vs. Being Effective

Would you rather be busy or effective? Look at 1 Corinthians 16:9: "For a great and effective door has been opened to me, and there are many adversaries." God wants us to be effective. Busyness is not necessarily effectiveness. Most people in America today are continually busy, but how many of these same busy people are really being effective for the kingdom of God? How many are just running here and there and everywhere doing anything and everything except what they're really supposed to be doing?

Ecclesiastes 10:10 says, "If the ax is dull, and one does not sharpen the edge, then he must use more strength; but wisdom brings success." Write this Scripture down and put it in a place where it will remind you that you can work busy, or you can work smart. If the ax is dull, it will continue to bounce off that tree. It takes a lot more strength and energy to get that ax through the wood.

A wise person will sharpen the ax head so he can get more done in a lot less time and with a lot less energy. "Wisdom brings success."

Years ago, when my wife and I were traveling in ministry, I came to a realization about my use of time. I was doing the church circuit, and my calendar was just about completely booked for a full year. But I knew I wasn't reaching as many people as I could. There were times when I would preach my heart out to two people at a time. Now I will preach as hard to two people as I will to 2,000 people. In fact, sometimes I preach a little harder to two people. We should give it everything we have to whomever we preach to. However, I was using up the same amount of time and energy to preach to two people as I was to preach to thousands at a time.

I prayed not just for doors to open, but for effective doors to open. I prayed for opportunities where I could minister to more people at once. Then the Lord opened the door for us to minister on TV. Now I can preach the Word on television, give an altar call, and reach over two million people on one program. That is effectiveness.

Don't just believe God for doors. Believe God for effective doors. My father-in-law, who is a Spirit-filled insurance salesman, told me, "Eastman, when you told me that, it really did something to me. I had been out knocking on doors, just beating doors down, but after you said that, I changed the way I was praying. I quit praying just for business. I started praying for good business. I quit praying just for doors to be opened. I started praying for effective doors to be opened. As I did this, the favor of God was all over me. I will walk into a place and in just two hours make the same amount of sales as I used to make in three full weeks!"

Those are effective doors. If you want to move forward in your destiny, you must be effective, not just busy. Do not let substitute activities bog you down. Keep your ax head sharp.

Other Things That Pull Us Off Track

I want to mention a few more things that can pull you off track and keep you from fulfilling your dream: people, an offended heart, and double-mindedness. These things can be like bullets trying to knock you down. You need to be aware of them and guard against them.

1. Other People

Every one of us has opportunities to be pulled off track by other people. Jesus was no exception. In the first chapter of Mark, Jesus experienced the temptation to be pulled away. The night before, He had cast out devils, healed the sick, and performed wonderful miracles. Early in the morning, while everyone else was sleeping, Jesus went off by Himself to find a quiet place to pray. When His disciples woke up and could not find Him anywhere, they started to panic. The whole city had come out to see Him, but where was He? The crowd was ready to keep the revival going. When they finally found Him, they said, "Everyone is looking for You" (Mark 1:37).

Isn't it amazing how when one or two people are doing something, it suddenly becomes "everyone"? Do you know what everyone is saying about you? Everyone thinks this! Everyone thinks that! Of course, the reality is everyone in the whole world is not saying or thinking all these things!

The disciples told Jesus, "Everyone is looking for You. What are You doing? We have a revival service going on. It is time to take an offering! We've got to have church!"

Jesus responded in verse 38: "Let us go into the next towns, that I may preach there also, because for this purpose I have come forth" (Mark 1:38).

Jesus knew His purpose. He knew what He was supposed to be doing, and no one was going to pull Him off course from that. He knew if He was going to finish what He had to do, He could not stay in one place. He had to move on to the other cities also.

We must do what God has put in our hearts to do. You may have people come and prophesy over you and speak different things over your life. I am all for true prophecy, but you really have to be careful sometimes, because this kind of thing can pull you off course if it is not from God. If someone gives you a personal prophecy that goes against everything God has already put in your heart to do, watch out.

Sometimes God will send someone to encourage you by confirming or clarifying some things He has already put in your heart. If someone starts telling you that you've got to do this and go here and do that, it needs to bear witness in your own spirit. It needs to be in line with what God has already put in your own heart.

If it does not, do not just run off and do it. It may pull you way off course and steal time that should have been spent doing what God told you to do. What happens when you get out there and things get tough? Where's that person who prophesied over you then?

2. An offended heart

The second thing that will taint your purpose is an offended heart. You can start out great: loving God, loving people, all fired up and full of determination to fulfill your dream. Then, someone does something dumb to you, and you slam on the brakes.

An offended heart can pull you off track quicker than a fly aiming for honey. You start to focus on the offense rather than on where you should focus your time and energy.

When someone offends you, just give it to God and trust Him to take care of it. Purpose in your heart to forgive them, keep right on loving them anyway, and move on. Climb right back on the road to your destiny. Do not let that offense pull at you and get you to give your attention to it.

"But you don't know what they've done to me," some people argue. No, maybe not. But I know what carrying an offense can do to you. I know how it can shipwreck your dream.

When you are tempted to hang on to an offense, you need to remember that it is doing you much more harm than the person who offended you. That other person is probably carrying on without ever once even thinking of what they did to you. They might not even realize that they offended you. Even if they did, they are not the ones getting all eaten up about it. You are the one who gets an ulcer over it. You are the one who gets high blood pressure over it. You are the one who has been stuck there, licking your wounds at the side of the road where you pulled off on the way to your destiny.

You have to choose not to be offended. It takes a quality decision. Sometimes you need to do something to help you move on. I have had people steal my offerings, and I had to send them money so I would not be offended. That will shut the devil up. Continue to pray for someone who has hurt you, and the devil will quit bugging you about it. He will quit bringing that before your eyes, because he knows that every time he flashes that thing up, you are going to do something good.

I have seen so many people who started out with the right motives and headed in the right direction. Then an offended heart caused their faith to suffer a shipwreck. Now they are not doing what God called them to do. They continue to look back over their shoulder to where they picked up the offense instead of looking ahead to where God wants them to go. You may not be able to change your past, but you can do something about your future. The choice is yours.

3. A double mind

Double-mindedness will confuse your purpose. It will cause you to lose your focus so that you can no longer go forward. The Word of God warns us about being double-minded. "For let not that man suppose that he will receive anything from the Lord; he is a double-minded man unstable in all his ways" (James 1:7,8). That word *unstable* in the Greek means "to roam around, to walk around, to have no purpose." It is hard to get anywhere if you have no purpose. Double-minded literally means two spirits. It suggests that you have different things going on at the same time.

The devil would like to destroy your vision by providing you with another vision. This splits your efforts and brings confusion so you don't know which way to really go. You work in one area a while, then go back over to the other area. Soon, you get so frustrated trying to accomplish two different things at once, you give up altogether. You become double-minded, unstable in all your ways, tossed back and forth.

When you know your focus, stay there. Don't get pulled off to the right. Don't get pulled off to the left. Stay focused on course.

It is great when you stay focused on your vision, when you keep moving along in your God-given destiny. Sometimes people are so caught up in doing the work and accomplishing their dream, that they forget what it is all about. The whole reason God gives you a vision is to advance the kingdom of God.

Thank God for your dream. Thank God for miracles. Thank God for all the great things He is doing in your life. Thank God for the healings and the financial breakthroughs. But don't forget what it is all about. God did not give you a dream to bless you and your family alone. He did not give you a purpose just to change your own world. What about changing the world? What about the harvest of souls?

Be focused, but don't forget the big picture. Remember the heart of God— which is to help people and to further His kingdom.

Chapter 9

Destiny Requires Passion

In Chapter Eight we talked about the importance of focus in order to obtain the vision God has for us. There is something else we need to accomplish our dream, and that is passion. Once you have discovered where your passion is (which we talked about in Chapter Two), you need to keep that passion stirred up. If you lose your passion, you stop moving toward your fulfilling your dream.

Passion is what gives life to your vision. Passion is the fire that fuels your dream and keeps you going. If you don't have any passion, it will be hard to stay focused. Without passion your vision becomes another good idea. I don't want to have just another good idea, only God ideas. I want to fulfill the dream and the vision that God has for my life. I want to be able to say with the apostle Paul, "I have finished my course with joy!" (Acts 20:24.) In order to do that, I have to have passion.

I would much rather work with someone who is uneducated but passionate versus someone who's loaded with education but doesn't have enough passion to blow out a birthday candle. I can do something with that passion. You can add knowledge and training to passion, but it is hard to put passion into someone who is like a dried up piece of wood.

Sometimes people with a bunch of fancy degrees and certificates and skills are the hardest ones to work with because they think they already have everything they need. But you take someone with a genuine passion for the things of God who has a sincere desire to learn and grow and advance in his or her calling, and you have someone who will go a long way. That is someone God can work with and make effective.

Now, zeal without knowledge is not good. The Bible talks about that in Romans 10:2-3. That can get some people off in ditches. Zeal with error can get you into trouble. I do not believe that you have to choose between zeal and knowledge. I believe you can have both. Zeal for God's Word and for the call He's given you, combined with knowledge of His Word and what He's given you to do, is a powerful combination.

When Jesus saw what the moneychangers were doing in His house, He got passionate. In John 2:17, it says that zeal for His house had eaten Him up. He was consumed with zeal for what He loved, and He got passionate when the people were abusing it. He grabbed a whip and drove out the moneychangers. He saw a bunch of religious stuff going on, things that were keeping people from a relationship with God, and it fired Him up. Jesus had passion for the things of God. He pursued His purpose with passion.

Serve the Lord Enthusiastically

In Romans 12:11 NLT, Paul tells us to "serve the Lord enthusiastically." Serve the Lord how? Enthusiastically. God wants us to serve Him with passion.

I have met people who believe it is a sin to show too much enthusiasm for the Lord. They become concerned if you get too excited for Jesus. I remember when I was preaching at a Church of God in the backwoods of southern Florida. The Lord was moving, and earlier that morning I had led a young man to the Lord, which not only fired him up, it fired me up too.

As I came into the sanctuary that evening, a lady greeted me at the door. She was a precious grandma with her hair stacked up very high with bobby pins and hairspray holding it all together. She said to me, "Young man, how are you doing today?"

I began to tell her what God had done, and how I had witnessed to a man at a dumpster and led him to the Lord right there by the dumpster. She got excited and began jerking and bobbing her head like a chicken. Bobby pins were flying out of the top of her head like scud missiles! The more Grandma shouted, the more I shouted. We stood there shouting and praising God together.

One of the deacons from the church came over. He was this great big man in a pinstriped suit with a big vest and his belly hanging over his pants. He walked up to me and said with one of those holy voices, "Ooh, friend. I used to be just like yooooou." When he said that, the thought went through my mind, *Oh, please. Tell me what happened to you so I never end up like you!* I mean, if he used to be just like me, what happened?

"And then I became mature in the Lord," he told me. And I thought, *Mature? Did you mean to say "manure"? Religion stinks.*

People will try to make you feel guilty for being enthusiastic. However, God wants us to be enthusiastic. It is His idea.

What the Romans Saw

The word enthusiasm originated in the early church during the time of the Romans. It comes from two Greek words, en, which means "within," and *theos,* which means "God." God within.

When the Romans saw the Christians, they looked up and said, "What's up with them? Why are they so happy?"

"Oh, they are Christians."

"Yeah, yeah, yeah. I know that, but why are they so happy?"

"Because Christians say God lives in them. And that's why they're so happy."

That is where the word *enthusiasm* came from: God within. God within us makes us happy. It stirs up a fire and a passion inside us and brings enthusiasm.

Now let me set the record straight. Your expression of enthusiasm may be different than mine because we are different people. Thank God that we are not all the same. Different people have different ideas about what enthusiasm is. For instance, my idea of enthusiasm is like, "Waaaaa!" When I get excited, I jump up and down, run, holler, scream, shout, and want to swing from a chandelier! That is my personality because I am wired to 220. Others may be wired on 110 and their idea of enthusiasm is "Mmm, mmm. Wow." And they may look like they are almost asleep. When they see me get excited, they think I have gone berserk. We are all wired a little differently.

However you show enthusiasm, just do it. The Bible tells us to "serve the Lord enthusiastically" (Rom. 12:11).

Maturing in the things of God does not mean you let your fire die. The Bible says the saints are preserved (Ps. 37:28), but it does not say anything about the saints being pickled. God does not want you walking around with a frown on your face. If anyone should be enthusiastic, it should be us believers. We not only have life, but abundant life! Healing, prosperity, and joy unspeakable have been given to us. That is not just in the life to come, but also in this life here on earth.

People in the world get excited. Just watch them at a football game or a concert. Come on! They know how to get enthusiastic about something they like. We have the right to be excited about what we like, and that includes our relationship with our heavenly Father.

Sometimes Christians are intimidated when they hear people in the world boast about how drunk they were, how hard they partied, fornicated, or committed adultery. They brag about it, and sometimes we can be intimidated and feel ashamed of righteous living. Turn that around and stand up for Jesus. He stood up for you.

Paul was ridiculed and persecuted, but he said in Romans 1:16, "I am not ashamed of the gospel of Christ, for it is the power of God to salvation for everyone who believes." Gospel means good news and is something we should get excited about.

One evening after a service, a young lady came up to me and said, "Eastman, I've got to tell you what happened. When you said to just go ahead and let it flow, to just smile and let it rip for Jesus and not to be intimidated, I took that to heart." She told me how every Monday morning the guys at school always talk about how they partied and who they took to bed over the weekend. "Well, this time," she told me, "I wasn't even gonna give them a chance."

When I went to my first class in high school on Monday, I sat down and said, 'Hey, I have to tell you what happened Sunday. God was moving! The power of the Holy Spirit was flowing! People were being saved and touched, man! It was great! We had a blast!' Then I tapped one of them on the shoulder and asked him, 'Hey, what'd you do over the weekend?' And they all just hung their heads. One said, 'I can't really tell you. I didn't do anything.'"

What is that? That is letting God within show. God wants you to be enthusiastic.

God Within Changes People

There is a natural enthusiasm people have. Anyone can be excited about something. When the Spirit of God fills you up with His fire and His passion, it is completely different. The enthusiasm that comes from God within can take a wimp and turn him into a warrior.

Peter said, "Jesus, I'll follow You wherever You go. I will do whatever You want me to do. I am going to stand with You, Jesus. I will never deny You. I'd die for You, Lord!" (Matt. 26:33,35 author paraphrase.)

Jesus looked at him and said, "Peter, before the cock crows three times, you will have denied me three times."

"Oh, not me," Peter said. "I'd never do that!" (Matt. 26:34,35 author paraphrase.)

However, when Jesus was arrested and taken away to be whipped, Peter's natural enthusiasm took a dive. When a handmaiden recognized him outside the court where Jesus was being tried, Peter's courage wilted. "Hey, didn't I see you hanging around Jesus? Wasn't that you I saw walking around with Him?"

"Lady, I don't know what you're talking about."

"It was you, wasn't it? Yes, I'm sure that was you."

"Woman, I'm telling you. I do not know what you are talking about. I do not know Him. It wasn't me!" In addition, he keeps denying that he has anything to do with Jesus. (Matt. 26:69-72.)

What happened to his earlier "enthusiasm" to do anything for Jesus? He wimped out because he hadn't been filled with the fire of God yet. He had not experienced that burning passion God puts inside each of us when He fills and empowers us with the Holy Spirit. He hadn't yet experienced God within.

Peter and the other disciples were filled with the Holy Spirit on the day of Pentecost: "And suddenly there came a sound from heaven, as of a rushing mighty wind, and it filled the whole house where they were sitting. Then there appeared to them divided tongues, as of fire...and they were all filled with the Holy Spirit and began to speak with other tongues, as the Spirit gave them utterance" (Acts 2:2-4).

It says that the Holy Spirit came to them as tongues of fire. When that Holy Spirit fire filled them, it burned away cowardice and replaced it with a Holy Spirit boldness. As that fire filled them up, it spilled out as a Holy Spirit passion. Then Peter stood up and preached. Now, this was the same guy who wimped out before, remember? He was the one who did not have the guts to admit that he even knew Jesus, much less that he was one of His disciples. Now he proclaimed the Word of God to the huge multitude of people who would come to find out what was happening.

It is not as if these people were all on their faces worshiping and praising God with them. No. They were saying, "Hey, what's with these people? What is all this blubbering about? What's going on? They must be drunk, that is what! Drunker than skunks!"

Peter didn't wimp out this time. The Holy Spirit fire was all over him. He was pumped. He was hot. He was filled with the passion of God. He preached Jesus with boldness as never before, and three thousand people were born again.

The God within made the difference.

Fuel Your Dream

Passion is the fire that fuels your dream and keeps you heading toward your destiny. If you want to reach your God-given dream, you need the passion of God. Stay pumped up with that Holy Spirit fuel. You won't get very far if you don't have passion.

God is looking for people who are ready to make it happen with enthusiasm, people with a passion to go all the way with Him. He is looking for people whose hearts delight in Him so that He can pour His burning desire into them and launch them into extraordinary things.

It's one thing to have that passionate desire burning in you, but it's another to keep it burning. If you are going to keep it burning, you have to stir it up. Paul told Timothy to "stir up the gift of God which is in you" (2 Tim. 1:6). Notice that he does not say that God will stir it up. He doesn't say, "Come here. Let me stir it up for you, Tim." No. He says that Timothy is the one who has to stir up the gift. So many times we are waiting for someone else to stir us up.

We want the worship team, the pastor, or a sovereign move of God to stir us up, but the Word of God tells us that we are the ones who are to stir up the gift in ourselves.

If you will learn this secret, you will be miles ahead of other people. Don't wait for anyone to do it for you. Don't wait for God to do it. He has already given you the gift. Now He expects you to do something with it!

When you stir up the gift in you, it causes others to become stirred up. Paul told the Corinthians, "Your zeal has stirred up the majority" (2 Cor. 9:2). When you are zealous, you are going to stir up the majority of people around you. You cannot help yourself. Zeal rubs off. It rubs off on others and stirs them up. I double-dare you to be stirred up and not stir up other people.

I remember one time when I was on an airplane flying from Billings, Montana, to Spokane, Washington—on one of those little puddle jumpers that goes up to its altitude, then comes right back down again. We were going down the taxiway, getting ready to take off, when a man yelled across the aisle, "Is that a Bible you're reading over there?"

It was 6:30 in the morning, and he hollered at me from across the plane. So I just looked over at him and said, "Yes, it is."

He jumped up—while we are on an active taxiway—and headed over to where I was sitting. "Praise God!" he beamed. "I just got saved and filled with the Holy Spirit. I was praying I'd get to sit next to a Christian."

When the flight attendant saw this man walking around while the plane was moving, she was concerned. "Sir! Please sit down! We're on an active taxiway!" If you want to upset a flight attendant, just stand up while the fasten seat belts sign is on.

This man just waved at the flight attendant, then sat down right beside me, buckled his seat belt, and proceeded to tell me how he had been born again. Here it was, 6:30 A.M., and this man was like a blazing fire of enthusiasm. He was just ripping. Pttrrrr... Rtatatat...PttrrrrRatatat! Just like a great big happy machine gun. He was so fired up.

Soon his enthusiasm got to me, and I became excited, too. I could not wait for him to be quiet so I could tell him what God has done in my life. The second he paused, I jumped right in. "Ha! You think that's great. Listen to this!"

The minute I paused, *boom!* He started again. We had church right there on Northwest Airlines. We were having a great time!

As the plane began to descend, a hand reached through the cracks of my chair, grabbed me by the back of the head, and started to pull my head. Someone jerked my head back. I turned to see who was doing this, thinking it was probably someone's little child who couldn't contain himself. But when I turned around, I saw a grandmother with a handful of my hair. I said, "Yes, ma'am, can I help you?"

"Are y'all Christians?" she asked.

Well, I guess somehow she had overheard us talking—along with the rest of the airplane. Before I could answer her, the man beside me blurted out,

"Christian! Yeah! Wowwww! Are you kidding?" And he started in so fired up that I had to interpret what he said.

"Yes, ma'am," I told her. "We are Christians."

So then she said, "Do y'all believe in miracles?"

"Miracles?" the man beside me howled. "Yeah! Wowwww!" Again he went berserk.

Again I had to interpret for him. "Yes, ma'am, we do believe in miracles."

"I need prayer," she said. "I got on this plane, and I have a sinus condition. It feels like my head is going to explode. Please pray for me."

"We'd love to." I reached into my backpack for the little jar of anointing oil I carry with me. At first, I just put a little dab on my finger. Then I remembered that she had told me she was Baptist. So I thought, *Well, praise God! Let's load her up.* So I just shook that whole thing out there and got a big Lake Superior in the palm of my hand. I took that anointing oil and plopped it on Grandma really fast.

Now, you have to picture this. I am in the bulkhead, which is at the front of the plane, so everyone is watching me. I'm getting ready to pray, and, honestly, I was going to just say the sweetest little prayer, the little God-move-on-granny prayer, when I feel this man put his hand on my back. No one can see him, but he begins to pray in tongues. He sounds like Yosemite Sam filled with the Holy Spirit. I am not kidding! "Yuh, yip a bu bu bu!"

He is screaming in tongues, and I have my hand on Grandma. Everyone is looking at me because they hear this eruption coming from the seat beside me. I just smiled and said, "Yeah, we're those people you've heard about. We are those radicals. That's us."

Then I thought, *He's letting it rip. I'm gonna let it rip, too.* So I grabbed her ears and started shaking, "Oh, God, just move on her. Oh, Lord, touch her." The man beside me was still ripping in tongues, praise God!

Then both of her hands shot up in the air and Grandma started to shout, "My ears! They popped open. Glory to God! I feel it! I feel it!" And she testified about how she had been healed on that flight, right there in front of everyone.

I wondered how everyone was handling this. I looked around at all these people looking at us. They looked at me, they looked at Grandma, and then they all started clapping.

There we were on Northwest Airlines on the 6:30 A.M. flight, having a revival! We had church! We had a testimony service. I preached a little bit. We had a healing line. We had a demonstration of the Holy Spirit. All we had left to do was pass the offering bucket.

When you are stirred up, you are going to stir up other people. Passion is contagious. When you are passionately pursuing the dream that God has placed in your life, it is going to affect others.

Give It Everything You've Got

If your passion dries up and your heart is not in what you are doing, you will not do it well. You will do just enough to get by. In fact, you will be tempted to quit altogether. When you have a passion for something, you put yourself into it. You live, breathe, think, and talk it. You give it everything you have. That is what passion does.

The Bible tells us to give ourselves fully to whatever we are doing. "Whatever your hand finds to do, verily, do it with all your might" (Eccl. 9:10 NAS). Don't do it halfway. Do it with all your might. There is something about being passionate about what God has called you to do. Maybe

He has called you to run a business. Run it with all your heart. If He has called you to be a doctor, do it with everything in you. In whatever God has called you to do—whether it is in your ministry, in your family, or in your profession—be passionate about it. Don't put in the minimal amount of effort. Give it all you have.

There are some things we should never get addicted to. We should never get addicted to anything that is potentially destructive to others or to ourselves. But there is one thing it is okay to be addicted to, and that is your calling. The Bible says that the house of Stephanas had "addicted themselves to the ministry of the saints" (1 Cor. 16:15 KJV). This is the only time this word is used in the Bible. They were addicted. That sounds like they were doing a little bit more than going through the motions of something. They were addicted to the ministry of the saints.

The most effective people in the kingdom of God are the people who are addicted to their calling. If God has called you to be an insurance salesman, be addicted to that call. Give it your focus. If God has called you to be a beautician, beautify to the glory of God. Whatever God has given you to do, do it with all your soul, strength, and might. You are not doing it unto men. You are doing it unto God.

It is your passion, your addiction. When you are addicted to something, everything else drops into the shadows. You want to feed your addiction. It does not matter how big or how small it seems. It is what you love to do. It is what God has called you to do, and that is your passion.

I have told God this: God, I don't care if I'm the water boy in the kingdom of God. I just want to be a part of this end-time harvest. Whatever you want me to do, I'm going to do it. You want me to scrub a toilet, I'll scrub toilets. You want me to run over here and help with this, I'll run over here. You want me to do this, that's what I'll do. If you want me to preach, I'll preach. I'll do whatever you want me to do, because I'm addicted to helping people.

If you want to fulfill your destiny, you need to keep the passion for it burning. You need to stir up the gifts God has given you and keep the fire hot. Don't let anything or anyone put the fire out. Let it burn. Let it blaze. Let its flames take you higher and further than you have ever gone before. Keep feeding the flames with the Word of God. Keep your passion burning with the promises of God for you. Keep the fire blazing with your words, your thoughts, your faith, and your actions. Keep the vision active. Keep it burning in your heart.

Chapter 10

Destiny Requires Faithfulness

Okay, so now you have big dreams. You have discovered what your God-given dream is, and you are pursuing it with everything in you. You have dared to do something new. You have written your vision down. You are talking about it, you are confessing the Word over it, you have taken steps to move into that dream, and you believe God for miracles to make it happen. You are focused, you are passionate, and you are ready to move forward into your destiny!

Then, all of a sudden, you find yourself stuck washing the dishes, scrubbing toilets, taking out the trash, and all the little mundane things in life. What do you do? You have a giant dream burning in you that is bigger than you are. You desire to teach the Word, but the only opportunity for you at your church is to work in the nursery. What do you do? You want to evangelize all over the world, but now you stay home and homeschool your children and help lead a study for teenagers. What do you do? You want to start a business, but you are working for someone else and helping him to grow his business. What do you do?

You are going to be faithful in the small things, that's what. Jesus taught us the importance of this. In Luke 16:10-11, He says, "He who is faithful in what is least is faithful also in much; and he who is unjust in what is least is unjust also in much. Therefore, if you have not been faithful in the unrighteous mammon, who will commit to your trust the true riches?"

Faithfulness is something you need in order to move forward into your destiny. It is a stepping stone to your dream, a proving ground. It is not just a place you have to pass through to get there. It is something you need to practice throughout your life. Be faithful with what you have, and God will bless you with more.

God Chooses the Faithful Ones

Paul Was Faithful

Paul the apostle said, "Jesus counted me faithful putting me in the ministry. I have been faithful with what I have been entrusted with. I've been faithful to do all that He called me to do." (1 Tim. 1:12; Acts 26:19.) Notice that Paul did not say that God counted him because he knew the Word forwards and backwards, or because he went to Bible school. He did not say God counted him for being charismatic, or for his great personality, education, background, or how much he spoke in tongues. No. The one characteristic he focused on was faithfulness. "God counted me faithful."

If you will be faithful to do what God has called you to do, you will see new realms and new dimensions open in your life. Seize the time and the opportunities that God has placed in your life. Be faithful in these things, and it will launch you into your destiny with fresh power.

Moses Was Faithful

Right after Moses had the burning bush experience, what did he do? He has just been in the presence of God on holy ground. God has spoken to him from a fire that does not destroy the bush. I mean, talk about a serious meeting with God! There is no doubt about it. It is a ten on the Richter scale. However, right after God commissions him to set the Israelites free from the captivity of Egypt, he goes back to his father-in-law and asks his permission to go to Egypt. "So Moses went and returned to Jethro his father-in-law, and said to him, 'Please let me go and return to my brethren who are in Egypt.'" (Ex. 4:18). He has just received his calling from the mouth of God, and he goes up to his father-in-law and says, "I know that I'm supposed to be tending the sheep, sir. But would it be okay if I go to Egypt to see my relatives there?"

There's not a lot of people who would bother checking with their boss after God has just given them a mandate to go somewhere on business for Him. It would be like if Jesus appeared to you with nail scars and told you to go to the President of the United States to turn the nation upside down for Him, but then you go to your boss and say, "Would it be okay if I head over there now?"

I believe that is one of the reasons God picked Moses for the job. Moses was faithful. He was a man of integrity. He was not the sort of man to take off without notice—even if God Himself had called him. Moses was faithful where he was, and God knew he would be faithful to do all that He had called him to do. God rewards faithfulness. When you're faithful, you can believe God's going to send some amazingly wonderful rewards your way.

David Was Faithful

> Now the Lord said to Samuel, "How long will you mourn for Saul, seeing I have rejected him from reigning over Israel? Fill your horn with oil and go; I am sending you to Jesse, the Bethlehemite. For I have provided Myself a king among his sons."
>
> 1 SAMUEL 16:1

When Samuel went over to Jesse's house to anoint the new king of Israel God had chosen, Jesse brought all his sons but one. So all these nice, tall young men passed in front of the prophet, Samuel. And since one of these men looked like a king to Samuel, he thought, *Surely this is the man. Surely this is the Lord's anointed.* (1 Sam. 16:6.) "But the Lord said to Samuel, 'Do not look at his appearance or at his physical stature, because I have refused him. For the Lord does not see as man sees; for man looks at the outward appearance, but the Lord looks at the heart.'" (1 Sam. 16:7). Despite how tall and great this man looked, God saw he did not have the kind of heart God was looking for. God had already chosen someone else with a different kind of heart: someone after His own heart.

Samuel told this man to move on. Then another man walked by and there was no direction from God. So Samuel said to Jesse, "Is this everyone? I'm not getting a witness here."

Then Jesse admitted that he had one other son, but he was out "keeping the sheep" (v. 11). Everyone else was trying out for their kingship, but David was keeping the sheep. He was doing what he knew to do. He was doing the job he had been given to do. Moreover, he was doing it with all his heart. He was faithful.

Samuel said to Jesse, "Send and bring him. For we will not sit down till he comes here" (v. 11). They went to get David and brought him before the prophet. As soon as he showed up, God said, "Arise, anoint him; for this is the one!" (v. 12). So Samuel took the horn of oil and anointed David as king.

This was David's moment. It was the moment God showed him his calling and his purpose. He was to be king of Israel. God ordained him for this. Wow! He is anointed to be a king! David didn't immediately go with Samuel and hang out at the king's palace.

In fact, King Saul was looking for a musician to play for him, so he commanded his servants to go get the little harp player he had heard about. "Therefore Saul sent messengers to Jesse, and said, 'Send me your son David, who is with the sheep'" (1 Sam. 16:19). David had just been anointed king, remember? But where was he? He was back with the sheep! That is faithfulness.

The Bible says that "the Spirit of the Lord came upon David from that day forward" (1 Sam. 16:13). God called David into his destiny that day because He saw that he was a man after His own heart. Deuteronomy 7:9 says that He is "God, the faithful God who keeps covenant and mercy for a thousand generations with those who love Him and keep His commandments." And in Revelation 19:11, He is "called Faithful and True." Repeatedly in the Word of God, God is described as "faithful." (Hosea 11:12; Heb. 2:17;10:23; 1 John 1:9; 2 Cor. 1:18; 1 Thess. 5:24; 1 Cor. 1:9.) God has a faithful heart, and He is searching for others with faithful hearts like His.

We can trust God because He has proven Himself faithful repeatedly. If we want to be successful in our calling, we need to prove ourselves faithful too. Even the world values faithfulness. No one wants someone who cannot be trusted. I want to be more like God. I want to be faithful, as He is faithful.

I believe the reason why David was a man after God's own heart was because he was faithful. He was faithful in what God had called him to be. God will pass over a million people to promote someone who is faithful. Proverbs 20:6 says, "Most men will proclaim each his own goodness, but who can find a faithful man?" God is looking for faithful people.

No Faithfulness, No Anointing

After David was anointed, something very significant happened. First Samuel 16:13 says that "the Spirit of the Lord came upon David from that day forward." Now look at the next verse: "But the Spirit of the Lord departed from Saul" (v. 14). Although David had been chosen and anointed by God to be king, Saul was still officially on the throne. God poured His Spirit out on David and took His Spirit away from King Saul. I believe He did that because David was faithful, but Saul was not. Saul didn't follow through on what God had instructed him to do. (1 Sam. 15:1-26.) He chose to be a people-pleaser instead of a God-pleaser. (1 Sam. 15:24.) He chose to exalt himself rather than to obey God. (1 Sam. 15:12.) Unfaithfulness caused God to remove His anointing.

Saul was still in the palace and David was still with the sheep. David didn't look like a king to anyone. He was not wearing all the royal garments yet. He was not operating in his calling yet. However, he was the one God anointed. David was not only full of faith, but he knew how to be faith-ful—even as God is faithful.

Sometimes there are people still in positions of authority who are no longer flowing in the anointing of God. They may still be preaching or teaching or holding crusades. They may still be running their businesses or ministries, but the anointing has lifted because they ceased to be faithful. Maybe, like Saul, they chose to please people more than God does. Maybe, like Saul, they started out well, but then they grew big in their own eyes. Samuel told Saul, "When you were little in your own eyes, were you not head of the tribes of Israel? And did not the Lord anoint you king over Israel?" (1 Sam. 15:17). I hate to say it, but sometimes this happens.

God is looking for faithful men and women to fulfill His plan for them. He is looking to pour out His anointing on those who are faithful to do all that He calls them to do. He is looking for people like David.

Be Faithful Where You Are

Maybe you don't have a dream of your own yet. Where are you working? What church are you involved in, and what is their vision? What is their mission statement? Find that out, then embrace it as if it were your own.

Then he broke down and told me, "Eastman, for years I have preached against contemporary gospel music. It is just not part of me. I don't believe in it. But you are ministering in contemporary gospel music and you are seeing results. To tell you the truth, I'm torn."

"So, would you rather I didn't do contemporary gospel music?" I asked him.

"Yes," he told me.

"Okay," I said. "That's all I needed to know. We will change."

Now, it is not that I was right and he was wrong. Our goals were the same, but the method to get to those goals was just a little bit different. I chose to submit and stay faithful under another man's ministry. I could have gone to our youth and said, "You know what? Pastor does not like contemporary gospel music. Can you believe it?" But I didn't. This is what I told the youth: "We are going to be changing some things around here. We are going in a new direction, and it is going to be exciting. We really feel that we're not to be heading in the direction of contemporary gospel music." Now, I did not feel that way. However, I did when the pastor felt that way because he was my boss.

I did not say "Pastor feels that..." or "Pastor says we can't go that way." I linked up with the pastor, because he was my supervisor and I was under his authority. If you work for someone, it is not about them versus you. They and I, they and I. That is how division comes in. It is hard to move forward when division is working against you.

When you get hold of the "we" vision, you grab the vision of your superior. You say, "This is the way we are going to do it," and watch what God will do with you. He is going to bless you.

I told our group, "Listen, we're going to move into Southern Gospel."

I heard the kids say, "Oh, Southern Gospel, ehhhhh! I hate that!"

"Hey! Knock it off! It is going to be good. I did not say it had to be like Southern. I just said we are going to sing Southern Gospel songs. We can make them funky. We can add a guitar and have a screaming guitar solo in the middle of some sax. It will be fun!"

If you can catch hold of that concept at your place of employment, or wherever God has you now, it is going to move you up. God wants to bump you up into leadership. It all begins with the way you perceive things. When you are faithful in what is another man's, God is going to give you true riches of your own.

Faithfulness Brings Favor

Look at what Paul told Timothy about the importance of faithfulness. "And the things that you have heard from me among many witnesses, commit these to faithful men who will be able to teach others also" (2 Tim. 2:2). Paul said to choose those who were faithful. He did not say they should commit these things to those with the most knowledge or experience. He did not say they should commit them to those with the most personality or eloquence. Faithfulness brings favor.

If you want to experience the favor of God in your life, you are going to have to practice faithfulness. I have noticed something about the people who have been exceedingly blessed in the kingdom of God. I have noticed that faithfulness is one of their essential characteristics. Faithfulness in what God has given you to do will cause God's favor to come on you and overtake you. If you are going to obtain the destiny that God has for you, it is going to require that you be faithful.

While my wife and I were attending Bible college, there were three men who were our friends and classmates. One of these guys was by far the most gifted of any of us. He could preach circles around any of us. He was an amazing communicator. He knew the presence and power of

God. He could play the keyboard and take you into the throne room of God in worship.

Out of the four of us, this guy is the only one who is not moving in his calling now. I pastor a church in Tulsa, Oklahoma. The other two are ministering, too. Our friend is still gifted, but he is not using those gifts for God. He has been through a couple of marriages and no longer attends church.

I am radical enough to believe that the gifts and calling of God are irrevocable. I believe that God's hand is still on my friend, and, as long as he has breath in his lungs, God is still calling him. There is much potential there. I believe that one day he is going to be the man of God that God has called him to be. What has kept him from succeeding?

Let me back up a bit and tell you what happened while we were working together in Bible school. Whenever there was an opportunity to minister somewhere, the rest of us grabbed any opportunity we could get. If someone said, "Hey, we need some help in the nursery," we would be there. We would get in there and change diapers. We were excited to have the opportunity to minister to these little kids that God had entrusted us with.

If someone said, "Hey, the baseboards in the youth room need cleaning," we would stay late to scrub them. We helped with the prison ministry in any way we could.

I noticed our friend would never do that. He would not even stoop down to pick up paper or hang around after church. He would wait for people to call him for an invitation to preach, and then they had to take care of his airfare and hotel. If they promised to receive a love offering for him, then he might think about going. That was when he was just starting out in ministry. He did not want to deal with the small details. He was not faithful in the small things.

The last time I saw him, he was all beat up. He was once one of the happiest people I ever knew. Now he is discouraged and depressed. He is not going to church. He is not ministering.

It has been said that the gifts will get you where you need to go, but your character will keep you there. You can have great gifts, you can be Mr. Personality, but your character will keep you in those high places.

The key to promotion is faithfulness. Faithfulness is what causes people to grow and to blossom in their calling. If you are not faithful in the small things, you are likely to stagnate or even regress.

While preaching in Grand Rapids, Michigan, I was getting ready to fly back home. We had already started the church here in Tulsa, so I was excited about coming home to preach on Sunday. Just before I left, the pastor of the church came up to me and said, "Eastman, I really want you to preach for me on Sunday morning. Would you mind doing that?"

Now, I love him. I enjoyed preaching at his church on Friday night and Saturday morning. However, I looked forward to preaching back home that Sunday. So I looked at him and said, "Pastor, I would love to, but we just planted a church in Broken Arrow. I am so excited about it. I get to go back and preach there tomorrow."

I could have chosen to preach there instead of my own church. Sure, in the short run, this looked like a better opportunity. It looks better to minister to thousands rather than hundreds. I would have probably gotten a bigger offering, too. But that would not have been the faithful thing to do. That was not what I knew I was supposed to do. I knew God had called me to look after the sheep in my fold. I am not doing it for the offering. I am not doing it for the numbers. I am doing it because that is where I am called. And that is where I am going to be faithful.

Jesus said, "If you have not been faithful in what is another man's, who will give you what is your own?" (Luke 16:12).

When you are faithful in what is another's, God is going to give you true riches of your own. When you are faithful in pouring yourself into whatever your hand finds to do now, God is going to pour out more blessings than you can hold.

Maybe you are working or serving somewhere where they don't do things exactly the way you would do them. What is the overall vision there? What is the main goal? Does it line up with yours? Then hook up with that. Learn from it. Give it your all. Be faithful there, and trust that God will honor that and move you to where you need to be at the right time.

When I was a youth pastor in Spokane, Washington, I saw God do some wonderful things. When I first arrived, we had 14 people in our youth group. Then we brought in contemporary gospel music, and the youth group began to explode. We prayed. We saw teens born again every week, and, within about three months, our youth group grew from 14 to 120. This was back in the early 80s, and that was a large number for a youth group.

God was blessing us, and I told the pastor what was going on. Whenever I shared with him about what was happening, he would get excited about the souls being saved and the people being touched, but then he would always look a little bit disappointed. I thought, *Well, he wants more people to get saved.* So we would have more outreaches. Our numbers continued to increase, and more people were born again. It was great. I would again share this with the pastor, but he would still look discouraged.

I really wanted to be under my pastor and be submissive to him, so one day I asked him, "Pastor, is there something wrong? Am I doing something that's not right?"

We may have started out small, but we have just exploded in growth since then. We have grown from hundreds to thousands in just a few years. It pays to be faithful. I have more fun preaching at our church in Tulsa than I do anywhere else in the world, because that is where God has called me to be faithful. God honors faithfulness.

Faithfulness Will Bump You Up

Faithfulness causes God to promote you. Notice that I said God will promote you. We do not promote ourselves in the kingdom of God. I know some people try to do this. Sometimes their efforts will get them to what looks like a higher position to men, but that is not God's promotion. Jesus said that when people do things to look good in the eyes of men, they already have their reward. (Matt. 6:2,5.)

Their reward is that people see them in the limelight here on earth. That is all they are going to get for a reward. However, when God promotes us, He showers us with more rewards than we can even dream of. I am not just talking about the rewards we will get in heaven. Yes, we will get our heavenly reward. But we'll also get heavenly rewards right here on earth while we're still busy moving in our destiny.

Faithfulness moved David to the throne of Israel. Faithfulness brought the promotion for the teachers of God's Word in Timothy's church. (2 Tim. 2:2.) Faithfulness moved the men with two talents and five talents into positions of rulership. (Matt. 25:21,23.) Faithfulness brought promotion for Joseph. (Gen. 39-41.) Despite the assaults against him, he remained faithful to God and to the dream God had given him. His faithfulness brought favor for him with men.

Despite Daniel's circumstances, he stayed faithful to his calling. He did not let anything or anyone keep him from the will of God for him. Even when his very life was threatened, he continued to pray faithfully as he had always done. (Dan. 6:10.) Faithfulness brought him favor with the king. (Dan. 6:1-3.) Daniel's integrity caused King Darius to select Daniel to be one of three governors over the 120 satraps, who were over the whole of Darius's kingdom.

Daniel 6:3 says, "Then this Daniel distinguished himself above the governors and satraps, because an excellent spirit was in him; and the king gave thought to setting him over the whole realm." Daniel continued to be promoted higher and higher because "an excellent spirit was in him." He was faithful wherever he served and bloomed wherever he was planted.

Character is greater than talent in the kingdom of God. God can add gifts and talents to character, but gifts and talents without character are empty motions without impact.

Character will promote you. Faithfulness will bump you up to a higher level.

Proverbs 25:19 says, "Confidence in an unfaithful man in time of trouble is like a bad tooth and a foot out of joint." Have you ever leaned on someone during a tough time, and then found out that person is unfaithful? You cannot depend on them. The Bible compares that kind of person with a rotten tooth or a foot that is out of joint. I think of pain. That is what an unfaithful person is like.

You cannot put any pressure on a broken foot, nor can you do that with someone who is unfaithful. If you begin to put pressure on a broken foot or rotten tooth, it will snap or crack. And, man, does it hurt! You cannot lean on someone who is unfaithful.

God is looking for people He can depend on. If He sees that you are not faithful in the small things, He will not give you greater things. He will not take you further into your destiny. He will not bring that dream in your heart to pass unless you are faithful.

There are some people who think that even if you have no ability, gifting, or anointing in an area, you will eventually succeed if you just stay faithful long enough. You may not be good at it, but if you will just keep doing it and working at it and practicing it long enough, you will eventually get good at it. However, that is not necessarily true. God wants us to operate in our giftings. Faithfulness alone is not enough to do it if you are not operating in the area God has called you into.

It amazes me how some people always want to do what they do not have a gift for. Have you heard certain preachers try to sing? I will get up and make a joyful noise to the Lord each week in church, but I do not claim to be a singer. I know that's not my calling, and I am not going to pretend that it is. However, I have been in services where the evangelist gets up and tries to sing. And I am thinking, *Oh, please, just preach, buddy. You are a great preacher! That is what you do well. But let someone else do the singing.*

Then again, sometimes you will hear great singers get up and try to preach. Now, I am not saying some singers cannot preach, but many times that is not their gifting. God called and anointed them to sing. I know some people are gifted in both, but often people are just trying to mimic someone else. They think that because everyone else around them is preaching, or because everyone admires preaching, they ought to get up and preach too.

You need to be doing what God has called you to do. If it is preaching, get up and preach with everything in you. If it is not, find out what you are supposed to be doing and do that. Don't try to do someone else's job. Don't think that if you are just faithful at something long enough, it'll automatically become your gift. That is not how it works. God has given you a gift that is all yours. It does not belong to someone else. It belongs to you. It is not meant for someone else to pick up and use. It's meant for you.

I remember when I was a youth pastor there was one little girl who wanted to be just like Amy Grant. She wanted to sing like Amy Grant. She wanted to look like Amy Grant. She wanted to be Amy Grant. She decided she wanted to get up in front of the youth group and sing. She came and we auditioned her. We listened to her and then said, "Go back and practice some more." She did that, and then she came back again. "Go back and practice some more," we told her. She practiced some more, then came back and sang for us again. "You need to take lessons," we told her. So she took lessons, then came back and tried it again. "Well, oh gosh, just keep practicing. Just practice some more."

After about eight months of that, we finally said, "Maybe there's something else that God is calling you to do." Then I began to encourage her. "Listen, you know what you need to do? You need to get out there and use the gift you have for conversation. You are great at conversation. You can talk to a doorknob and make that doorknob feel great. I would love it if you would greet people at the door. You would be great at that. Would you do that for me?"

That is what she did. She changed the whole environment of the youth group when she was greeting people at the door. The people came in expecting to see her. She knew how to make them feel warm, welcome, and excited. Even before we played one note on the keyboard or sang one song, they were fired up. They were happy. They were encouraged and ready to receive. The difference was that this girl was now moving in her gifts. She was using the gift God gave her instead of trying to use someone else's gift. Now this girl is in ministry, traveling around and blessing people with her gifts. That is what I love to see. I love to see people using their gifts for God.

When David was told to put on Saul's armor to fight Goliath, he tried it on but realized that it just did not fit him. He was not comfortable in another man's suit. He could not move freely in it. David handed it back and said, "No thanks. That is not me. That belongs to Saul." (1 Sam. 17:39.) David knew that if he was going to succeed for God, he had to be who God made him to be. We need to be who God intended for us to be instead of trying to copy others.

The Bible talks about how God gives different people different gifts (1 Cor. 12), and how He makes some people rulers over tens, some over hundreds, and some over thousands. (Ex. 18:25.) Some are great captains over tens, and they are just as important as the people who are captains over hundreds and thousands. God needs you to take your place in the body of Christ. He needs you to do what He's called and assigned you to do.

If you don't do your part, there will be a gap. If you're busy trying to be someone else, then you're not going to be any good at what you're really supposed to be doing.

God wants us to be faithful to use the gifts He's given us. Your calling is important, but the gifts that God gives you are going to make up that calling. When God calls you to do something for Him, He also gives you the gifts and the abilities to do it. You need to match both the gifts and the calling. When you mix faithfulness with the giftings God has given you and apply them to your calling, you have a recipe for success, and you will see the power of God released in your life.

Feet on the Ground, Eyes on Your Dream

It is easy to become so caught up in tomorrow that we forget where we are today. I used to work with a person who was always so preoccupied with thinking about his tomorrow that if you tried to carry on a conversation with him, it was as if he were not even there. People like that are not living in today because they have already moved into tomorrow.

Once God begins to show you what He has in store, you can get so excited about where you are going that you do not put anything into where you are now. We must remember that in order to reach tomorrow, there are some things that you have to do today. You must stay faithful where you are if you want to get to that place God is preparing. Do not forget about your vision, but keep aiming for your dream.

We need balance. We must keep our feet on the ground without losing our vision for tomorrow. Be faithful with what God has placed in your hands right now, and get ready for promotion. Advancement is on the way.

Ecclesiastes 9:10 says, "Whatever your hand finds to do, do it with your might." When you find something to do, do it with all your might. The New Testament reference to this is found in Colossians 3:23. The New Living Translation says, "Work hard and cheerfully."

Do you work hard? Do you work cheerfully? The sad truth is that a lot of people will walk up to their place of employment, and the minute their hand touches the door, they wilt. *Ohhhhh, they sigh. I have to go to work. Gotta do the 9 to 5 grind again. Oh, boy. Here we go.* They walk in and it is like they are dead. They just go through the motions, just try to get through another day, just try to do whatever has to be done to make it. It is as if they are sleepwalking. They do not come alive until they walk out that door again. They live for Friday, and you don't see a spark in them until the weekend finally gets there.

What would happen if we rolled out of bed on Monday morning with this attitude? "Oh, glory to God! It is Monday morning. I get to go to work! Praise the Lord! It's time to go to work!" I guarantee your whole outlook would change.

Faithful people are not afraid to work hard wherever they are. Faithful people do not work hard and cheerfully only when they are doing what they like to do. They work hard and cheerfully wherever they are working—even if it is not their cup of tea. They give it their best. They give it everything they have because they are faithful.

Be faithful where you are. Work hard and cheerfully at whatever you do, and promotion will come.

Do It as Unto the Lord

Bondservants, obey in all things your masters according to the flesh, not with eyeservice, as men-pleasers, but in sincerity of heart, fearing God. And whatever you do, do it heartily, as to the Lord and not to men, knowing that from the Lord you will receive the reward of the inheritance; for you serve the Lord Christ.

COLOSSIANS 3:22-24

People are not always going to slap you on the back and say, "Hey, you're doing a great job!" They may not pay you as much as you would like. They might not even notice all the extra things you do behind the scenes. However, you are not working for people. You are working for God. And God sees everything. He is the One who is going to praise you and reward you, so look to Him instead of people. When you do this, you are not going to wait to kick into high gear until the boss is around, because you know that your real Boss is God and He is always around.

A few years ago, our church staff would act busy when they knew my wife, Angel, was pulling into the parking lot. This was so funny to me. As I was working in my office, I would hear an announcement, "Everyone, can I have your attention? Angel is in the parking lot. Look busy!" Then I would hear all these papers start to shuffle, and I would just crack up about that.

We are working for God, and He rewards your faithfulness whether people are watching or not. Be faithful where you are, "knowing that from the

Lord you will receive the reward of the inheritance; for you serve the Lord Christ" (Col. 3:24). God is a great employer! He will take care of you.

The Bible tells us in Hebrews 6:10 that God will not forget your labor of love. He has a great reward for you—not just in the hereafter, but right here on earth! Your payday is coming! If you have sown some things, you have a harvest to bring in. Maybe you have given into some businesses or done some things in churches or ministries. You have given your money, your time, and your talent. Maybe no one has ever noticed, but God noticed. He has rewards for you, and payday is coming as long as you stay faithful. Payday is coming as long as you keep a good attitude and look to God as your Source of supply. God pays His workers well!

Jesus tells us a story in Matthew 25 about three different men. Two of them are faithful to do something with what their master gave them, but one is not. The story begins in verse 14, where we learn that the first servant is given five talents which he develops and multiplies. The second servant is given two talents which he is faithful to do something wonderful with. The third man is afraid to do anything at all with his one talent, so he buries it in the ground.

When their master gets back, the first two men show him what they have done with what he gave them. And he says, "Great job, guys! You both did well! You were faithful over a few things, so now I'm going to make you ruler over many things." (Matt. 25:21.) Then he sees the other one who has just been sitting there all this time doing nothing at all with what he was given, and he gets upset. "Why didn't you at least go put what I gave you in the bank, man?" he tells the man. "Then at least it would have earned some interest for me." So then he takes his talent away and gives it to the first man who doubled his five talents.

Which one are you going to be like? What do you want your Master to say to you? I know that I want Him to say, "Well done, good and faithful servant; you were faithful over a few things, I will make you ruler over many things" (Matt. 25:21).

If that is what you want, then you are going to have to be faithful in whatever you have to work with.

The Same Reward

I want you to notice something about this story in Matthew 25. Look at what happens when the master comes back and starts handing out praise and rewards to those who have been faithful to use and multiply what they started out with. Look what he says to the man who had been given five talents. "His lord said to him, 'Well done, good and faithful servant; you were faithful over a few things, I will make you ruler over many things. Enter into the joy of your lord'" (v. 21).

To the man who had been given two talents he says, "Well done, good and faithful servant; you have been faithful over a few things, I will make you ruler over many things. Enter into the joy of your lord" (v. 23). Did you notice that the master said the exact same thing to the man who started with five talents as he did to the man who had been given two talents? Both of them received the same reward. The man with only two talents got the same praise and the same reward as the man who had five. They were not rewarded according to how much talent and ability they had been given to start with. They were rewarded according to what they did with what they had, and their master rewarded that faithfulness equally.

This story is a picture of our Master and Lord and how He rewards our faithfulness. If you are faithful to do all that God has given you to do, you will get the same reward as I do for being faithful to do all that God has given me to do. It does not matter if you are counting envelopes in the back room after service, or if you are up on the platform preaching. It does not matter if you are hidden away in a closet praying your heart out for souls to be saved in South Africa, or if you are out there holding crusades and getting a million natives saved. What matters is your faithfulness. If you have been doing what you were called to do, your reward will be the same.

If you will get this concept, it will change your life. Many times people get it in their heads that in order to really be rewarded they have to be the man up at the front. That is not what the Word says. The Word says that when we are faithful with whatever we have been given, we will get the same reward from God. The man in the parking lot who's waving his hands, smiling, giving people high-five's when they get out of the car, and saying "Great to see you!" gets the same rewards I get when I'm ministering, when I give an altar call, and when people are born again, because he is faithful to do what God has called him to do.

It is not about how many talents you have to start with. It is about what you do with what you have. It is not about who is in the limelight the most, or who preaches the most, or who has the biggest ministry or career, or who looks the greatest. It's about being faithful to do whatever God has given you to do. When you catch on to this, you are going to enjoy what God has called you to do much more.

The Greatest Reward

I once met a man on an airplane who asked me, "I know you're a dreamer. I like hanging around you. But when it's all said and done, what do you want to have accomplished?"

I looked at him and thought for just a second. Then, from the bottom of my heart, I said, "When it's all said and done and I've finished everything, I want Jesus to say to me, 'Well done, good and faithful servant. You have been faithful over what I've called you to do.' That's what I want most." To me, that will be the greatest reward of all.

Unfortunately, He will not be able to say that to everyone. The Bible says that Jesus is going to turn away from some who think they did all kinds of wonderful things for Him. Look at what Jesus says in Matthew 7:21-27:

> Not everyone who says to Me, "Lord, Lord," shall enter the kingdom of heaven, but he who does the will of My Father in heaven. Many will say to Me in that day, "Lord, Lord, have we not prophesied in Your name, cast out demons in Your name, and done many wonders in Your name?" And then I will declare to them, "I never knew you; depart from Me, you who practice lawlessness!"
>
> Therefore whoever hears these sayings of Mine, and does them, I will liken him to a wise man who built his house on the rock: and the rain descended, the floods came, and the winds blew and beat on that house; and it did not fall, for it was founded on the rock.
>
> But everyone who hears these sayings of Mine, and does not do them, will be like a foolish man who built his house on the sand: and the rain descended, the floods came, and the winds blew and beat on that house; and it fell. And great was its fall.

Notice the key in these verses: faithfulness. Jesus compares those who do His will with those who do not. There are rewards for faithfulness and obedience. Some people who think they are going to get these fantastic rewards and all kinds of praise from Jesus are in for a big surprise, because He's going to say, "I never knew you."

Well, I do not know about you, but I want to do all the will of God. I want to accomplish all that He has for me in my destiny. I want to say with the apostle Paul, "I've run my course. I have finished my race. I have done everything God called me to do, and I have done it with passion, with joy, and with the power of God. I've done it cheerfully, not as working for men, but as unto the Lord." (Acts 20:24; Eph. 3:7; 2 Tim. 4:7; Col. 3:23.)

If you will have that attitude, just watch. Your payday is coming. If you do not grow weary in well doing, you will reap your harvest. You will not faint. You will be refreshed.

If you will be faithful to do all that God has called you to do, God is going to promote you and reward you. He is going to bump you up to a higher level. He is going to take you into new realms and new dimensions of His glory. Do not grow weary on the way. Keep pressing in. Keep advancing in your destiny, and know that God has empowered you to succeed in all that He's called you to do.

Chapter 11

Roadblocks, Detours, and Wrecks

Okay, so now you're on your way. You have discovered your dream. You have taken steps to get there. You are focused, you are faithful, and you are passionate. You are seeing miracles. You are heading full force toward your dream. You are moving in your destiny.

What happens when you come up against a roadblock or a detour? What do you do if you hit something in your way, and *bam!* Your dream looks like it has been totaled. Do you quit?

Have you ever been on an airplane when they've said, "We're sorry, but the towers put us in a holding pattern." Then, for fifteen or thirty minutes, you are just flying in a circle. One time I was in a holding pattern for two hours on an airplane. That is a long time just to be flying in circles.

Sometimes we can feel like we are in a holding pattern in our lives. We feel like we are going in circles instead of moving forward in our destiny. What do you do when that happens?

First, you must realize that delays happen. Don't immediately assume that just because you are experiencing a delay or some sort of obstacle, you are going the wrong way. That is possible, but don't assume that. Find out. In order to do that, you need to know where the delay is coming from and why. There are three sources of delays: (1) delays caused by God; (2) delays caused by the devil; and (3) delays we cause.

Three Sources of Delays

1. Delays From God

God can keep us in a holding pattern because He has a right time for us. Sometimes things need to happen before we are ready to step into that calling. Preparation time is needed.

Moses went through a time of preparation for forty years when he was in Pharaoh's army. He learned a lot of strategy there. Those forty years were not wasted. God used that time to prepare Moses for his calling. After that, he spent the next forty years ministering to a bunch of sheep. That takes some effort to do that kind of stuff, you know. But the whole time he was working under the Pharaoh, and while he was tending those sheep, God was preparing Moses for great things.

Jesus went through times of preparation. He prepared thirty years for three years of ministry here on earth. Sometimes we send people out after just three years of Bible college and think that is enough to prepare them for thirty years of ministry. Jesus went through thirty years of preparation time.

The apostle Paul spent an entire year in the wilderness before he started moving into his calling. Before that, he had learned some things as a Pharisee that were part of his preparation for ministry. He studied the Torah and began to glean some things from God's Word. He was being prepared. The Bible tells us that "it is God at work in [us] both to will and to do of His good pleasure" (Phil. 2:13). God is continually preparing us for our destiny.

When I was ten years old, my dad bought me a shotgun. I was so excited, because I knew this meant I could go hunting with him. However, my dad did not just hand me a shotgun one day unexpectedly and say, "Okay, kid, go start blowing some stuff up." If he had done that, I probably would not be standing here today. No. My dad prepared me for that shotgun ahead of time. I did not start out with a shotgun. I started out with a Red Ryder BB Gun. It was while I used that BB gun that my dad taught me the Ten Commandments of gun safety. He taught me how to keep my BB gun clean and not to aim it at anyone. After I learned how to handle that BB gun responsibly, my dad gave me a .22. It wasn't until I had learned how to shoot that .22, that he finally gave me a .410 shotgun. Then I could hunt with him.

God prepares us for things one step at a time. You are who you are today because of the preparation that you were getting yesterday. God is continually preparing us for the next step we are to take. Sometimes even the experiences we would never guess God could use are used to prepare us for our destiny. When I was training ducks at my dad's tourist attraction, God was training me for ministry. When I was doing bird shows, He was working on my communication skills. When I was pulling weeds, He was teaching me diligence and perseverance. Every step of the way, God was always working on me. God is continually preparing us for increase, growth, and development so that we can fully and successfully complete His plan for us. He knows when we are ready for the next step. He knows the right time for each step.

When I first started in ministry, I did not just start speaking in churches. The first time that I really began to minister was when I began a little Bible study at my school. I was the only professing Christian out of 326 students, so I guess that qualified me to teach a Bible class. Then I hooked up with our local church and started playing drums every Sunday for each of the five services they had. (Yes, they had five services every Sunday!)

As the church grew, other musicians came in, so I needed to rotate with others who wanted to play. Even when I was not playing drums, I would help wherever help was needed.

All this time, I knew God had a call on my life for ministry. I was being prepared, and I knew I needed to be faithful where I was. I would go to church whether I felt like going or not. I did not wake up and say, "Do I feel like church today or not? Oops, got a hangnail. Maybe I'd better not go today." No. I didn't think like that. I just said, "Bless God, I'm going to church!" I was committed and was going to be faithful in the small things.

One day the College and Career teacher was sick. So he called me up and asked me if I would teach his class that week. I said, "Yes, I would be glad to do it." But, on the inside, I was saying, *Oh, my Lord! I have never done this before. How am I ever going to do it?* However, I agreed to do it, so I got ready. I prayed. I got my Bible out and was giving it all I could to prepare for that class. Then, when I got up there in front of that class, I thought, *Okay, here we go.* I was so nervous that it took me all of three minutes to get the whole message out. Just *bloop,* and I was done. (Those days are gone forever! I don't know where those three-minute messages went, but I haven't seen them since!) Well, when my message was done, I thought, *What now?* So then I gave an altar call, and people were born again. I laid hands on the sick, and people were healed.

The College and Career teacher moved elsewhere, so I was asked to take over the class. I was so excited for the opportunity, and I accepted. Every week I would minister the Word of God there faithfully. While I was teaching there, a man from the Full Gospel Businessmen's ministry heard that things were happening in my class, so he asked me to speak at one of his meetings. Well, I was both excited and nervous. I had never spoken in front of a big crowd of people I had never met before. But I said, "Yes, I'll do it."

I was moving closer and closer to my destiny, when, suddenly, they just quit asking. So I invited myself. I would go to rollerskating rinks because I knew there would be people there. Wherever people were, that is where

I went. I introduced myself. "Hi. I am a motivational speaker. May I talk to the owner?" I would talk to the owner. "Say, listen. You have many kids in here. I would love to talk to them about staying off drugs, keeping clean, and going for their dreams and visions. Would you mind if I talked to them?"

"Oh man, these heathens, they need help. They tore up my machine back there. Yeah, sure. Tell them all you want to. Just go ahead."

Then I would ask, "Would you mind if I pray?"

"Oh, go ahead. Pray. Whatever you need to do. They just need help."

I would get up there and preach at the rollerskating rink. I'd call everyone together, give out a few things, then I'd stand up and say, "Before I give out this last thing, I want to tell you a little bit about...." Then I'd give a five-minute message and an altar call, and kids would receive the Lord. I would go out there every Saturday and speak, and people would get born again every week.

After that I started going to prisons and jails and wherever I could minister. Eventually I went on the road as an evangelist, traveling all around the country for seventeen years. That entire time God was preparing me to pastor. Now, that doesn't mean that everyone who starts out teaching Bible classes or doing traveling ministry is destined to pastor. I know there are pastors who are being prepared for the road. Brother Kenneth Hagin pastored for many years before God moved him into his true calling as a teacher. But there is always preparation time involved in our getting to our destiny. God prepares us for our calling. And that takes time. It takes time to develop and mature. Even the apostle Paul didn't jump right into his calling the day he was born again.

Sometimes delays come because we are just not ready to handle what God has in store for us yet. I don't believe that ten years ago my wife and I would have been able to handle the things that are happening in our ministry today—even though I had these things burning on the inside of me back then. There was a right time.

Habakkuk 2:3 says, "For the vision is yet for an appointed time." God has an appointed time for you, but you have to stay steady. "Though it tarries, wait for it; because it will surely come." You have to know that it will surely come. However, there is an appointed time. So what do you do until then? You stay faithful where you are. Philippians 1:6 says, "Being confident of this very thing, that He who has begun a good work in you will complete it until the day of Jesus Christ." God is going to finish the work that He starts. He is not just a starter. He is a finisher. He completes the work He has begun on the inside of us.

Many people these days are in such a hurry for everything. If they cannot microwave it, they do not want anything to do with it. However, God has something better for you than just a microwave thing. Sometimes it is a slow burn, a slow cook. Don't things taste better from the oven or a slow cooker than they do from a microwave? Some things you just cannot microwave if you want them to turn out right.

Acts 17:26 tells us that God has a pre-appointed time for each of us. I like the way the New International Version says it: "And [God] determined the time set for them and the exact places where they should live." Not only does God have a time for you, but He also has a place for you. I do not know if you have ever been at the wrong place at the wrong time, but it is no fun. I heard one pastor make this statement: "If you're an evangelist, it really doesn't matter where you live. Now, if you are not an evangelist, it does matter. But if you're an evangelist, you can be satisfied anywhere you are."

As an evangelist, I have based my ministry out of the wrong place at the wrong time, and it is not okay. It does matter where you live. God has an appointed time and an appointed place for you. God had you on the blueprint before creation. He knew your gifts, your calling, and the deposit He was going to put in your life. So He said, *Where will they be most effective this time?* In addition, He predetermined where you were to live and when you were to do what you are to do. You may have started heading to a specific area to go to school or for a job, but if you are not running in rebellion from the plan of God, He may well have something there for you that you never even knew about. I have found out that we should never move unless or until God says, Go. God knows where we are to live.

2. Delays From the Devil

Not all delays are from God. Some delays are from your enemy, the devil. First Peter 5:8 says, "Be sober, be vigilant; because your adversary the devil walks about like a roaring lion, seeking whom he may devour." The Word calls the devil your adversary. He roams about looking for any opportunity he can find to get to you. Many times he will try to put up blockades to keep you from moving forward in the call of God. He will try to get you to crash your dream. If he can't get you to stop or give it up altogether, he'll try to send you off on some wild detour that will delay the plan of God. He'll use different situations, circumstances, or other people to try to prevent you from fulfilling your dream.

The devil will bring people across your path just as God brings people across your path, because just as God has a plan for you, so does the devil. So don't think he's about to let you fly into your destiny without any attempts to botch it up. The devil does not want you to be effective in what God has given you. But guess what? You get to choose which plan you are going to fulfill: God's or the devil's. The devil will try to put up a roadblock to God's plan, but that does not mean you cannot blast it out of the way. He will try to pull some tricks, but that doesn't mean you have to fall for them.

Some people think that the only time we come up against a full-blown attack from the devil is when we have done something wrong. Sometimes he will come against you just because you are doing something right. You need to understand that he is trying to stop you from obtaining your God-given dream. Do you know what the devil's job description is? Steal, kill, and destroy. That is what he does. He will destroy, kill, and steal from anyone who will let him. He is out to destroy the plan that God has laid out for your life. He's out to steal your purpose and kill your dream.

Paul said in 1 Corinthians 16:9 that "a great and effective door" had been opened to him. Not just a door, but an effective door. He goes on to say this: "And there are many adversaries." Even though God is opening up a great and effective door for you, there's someone on the other end of that door trying to push that thing shut to keep you from walking through it! When you start moving toward the plan of God, do not be surprised when opposition comes. Things will try to prevent you from fulfilling your dream.

But a lot of people lay down and say, "Well, I prayed for God to open up a door that no man can close, and to close doors that no man can open. Whatever happens, happens. If it doesn't happen, I guess it's not meant to be." No! Sometimes the enemy is on the other end of that door, and you have to kick that door open in the name of Jesus! You have to blast through that thing with the power of God and knock the door open! Just because it looks like the door is shut does not mean that God shut it. Sometimes your opponent has slammed that thing shut.

You have to be tenacious. You have to keep knocking, keep kicking at it, and keep beating at that thing. Eventually, that door God gave you is going to open. Now, if you've been trying to kick the same door open for twenty years without success, it may be time to consider whether it's really a door God has given you to walk through. Sometimes we can assume we are supposed to go a certain way, but it might not be the way God has for us. As I said earlier, some delays can be a matter of God's timing. Then again, sometimes we are the ones who put up barriers. I will talk more about that later. But if you know it's something God wants you to do, then you need to push through the barriers, because God doesn't bar doors that He's given for you to walk through. That is what the devil does.

When you start heading into your destiny, often all hell will break loose. Why? If the devil can nip your dream in the bud, you will never fulfill it. If he can whip you before you ever really get started, then he will not have anything to worry about. Don't let him do it. God has called you to be more than a conqueror. (Rom. 8:37.) Not just a conqueror, but more than a conqueror! "Thanks be to God who always leads us in triumph in Christ" (2 Cor. 2:14).

3. Delays We Cause

Sometimes delays have nothing to do with either God or the devil. Have you ever noticed that the devil gets credit for a lot of stuff? Our own flesh can do a lot more damage to our dreams than the devil tries to do. Many times it is easier to blame God or the devil for not accomplishing our goals. "Oh, that old devil's messing with me again!" Or, "Well, it's just not God's time yet." So we excuse our not getting on with what we're supposed to be doing by saying it's either the devil's doing or God's. More often than not, we are the ones who cause most of our delays.

It can be our own attitudes, the way we think, or the things we say that create barriers to our destiny. We talked about watching what we say, feel, and think in Chapter Five. In Chapter Eight, we talked about how distractions and substitute activities can pull us off course. We also talked about how circumstances can keep us from progressing in the plan of God.

There are things that can create roadblocks or detours—things that have to do with our own flesh. Some things that can hold us back include: fear, unbelief, pride, immorality, disobedience, confusion, discouragement, laziness, greed, impatience, taking offense, or wanting to please others more than God. Then again, sometimes we experience delays just because we make poor choices.

Why We Cause Delays

Fear

Our own fear can hold us back from our dreams. Fear of change, fear of failure, fear of disapproval, fear of the unknown. Fear can paralyze us and keep us from being effective in our calling. Fearful thoughts can come up as barriers to our progression. We start thinking that we cannot do it. What if this happens?

We must stop these thoughts from taking root in us, or they will freeze us where we are. When those thoughts of fear become words of fear, we are really in trouble. We talked about what our words and thoughts can do in Chapter Five. They can either launch us into our destiny, or they can put up blockades.

So what do you do when you feel fear rising in you? Instead of thinking thoughts of fear, you need to turn that whole thing around and start thinking faith thoughts. *I'm not going under. I'm going over. I'm not going down in defeat. I'm blasting up in victory. I'm not backing up. I'm pressing in. I'm not going down. I'm going forward in what God has for me.* You have to fight fear with faith, because faith is the opposite of fear. Besides that, God tells us 366 times in His Word not to be afraid—that is once for every day of the year plus an extra time for leap year. God does not want us to be bound up by fear. He wants us to be freed up by faith. Faith pleases God. "Without faith it is impossible to please [God]" (Heb. 11:6). When you're busy thinking faith thoughts, you're too busy to think fear thoughts.

Isaiah 26:3 reminds us that God will keep us in perfect peace when our mind is stayed on Him. You cannot hold both fear and peace at the same time. So what does that do? It gives the devil one up. Do not let the devil steal your peace. Don't let him distract you from God and His plan for you. We have victory over fear. Purpose to keep your mind on the Lord. God's job is to keep you in peace, but it is your job to keep your mind stayed on Him. When you are tempted to get discouraged, say, "Nope. My mind is stayed on Him." Then focus on the Lord and His Word and His promises.

Don't ever let the devil convince you that it is too late to get your mind back on God once you have veered over into fear. It's never too late to turn back to God. If you have found that you have given into anxiety, you can still move off that route and get back on the track of faith. But you have to make a choice to do this. It's not going to happen automatically. You have to get your mind to think about the things of God. Meditate on the Word of God. Speak out the promises of God. Proclaim them. Fill your mouth with the praises of God. Sing! Rejoice! Dance! Laugh! March around the house singing and proclaiming the truth of God. Fix your heart on the goodness of God.

When you stay focused on God and His Word, you will not have room for all that other nonsense. Do not let the devil or anything else steal your peace. No matter what you are going through. No matter what bombs are blowing up beside you. No matter what circumstance or situation you are in, determine in your heart that you are not going to let anything pull you off course.

Discouragement

There are always opportunities to get discouraged. You can get discouraged because of what other people have said to you, or because someone you look up to does not look up to you or did not smile when you walked by. You can get discouraged when you don't follow through on a goal you set for yourself or when things don't work out the way you thought they would.

However, discouragement can pull us off course. Have you ever tried to walk somewhere with your head hanging down and your eyes on the floor? Not only is it hard to move forward at a decent pace that way, but it is dangerous. If you do not look up, you are likely to bump into something and get hurt. If you want to keep progressing in the plan of God, you've got to learn how to bypass those opportunities for discouragement. You've got to learn how to make lemonade out of the lemons that come your way.

You choose what is going to come out of your mouth. You choose what you're going to look at. When it looks like you're not going to make it, say, "God always causes me to triumph in Christ Jesus!" (2 Cor. 2:14.) When it looks like you are going under, get up and shout, "Thanks be to God who gives me the victory through my Lord Jesus Christ!" (1 Cor. 15:57.) When you feel like you want to cry, sing! Rejoice in God, knowing that He is going to supply all your needs according to His riches in glory. (Phil. 4:19.)

Laziness

"The soul of a lazy man desires, and has nothing; but the soul of the diligent shall be made rich" (Prov. 13:4).

Sometimes we procrastinate because we are lazy. We are cruising through life. We don't want to put in the effort it takes to get to our destiny. We don't want to bother with adjusting to some changes. We do not want to invest in the extra work it will require. We are too comfortable where we are. We like it where we are, and we do not want to move out of our comfort zone.

I often say, "Misery is a great motivator." Sometimes it takes getting miserable enough where we are to be motivated enough to get up and do something different. If you are tired of always fighting with your spouse, what do you do? You pick up books. You read about how to improve your marriage. You go to seminars. You pray. You seek counseling. You do something about the situation. Misery will motivate you to take a step.

God doesn't want us to strive in our own flesh to accomplish His will. He does not want us to try to do it all by ourselves. But neither does He want us to just sit there waiting for our dream to leap into our lazy laps. God gave us legs to do something with. He gave us hands to do something with. He says in His Word that He will "bless all the work of your hand" (Deut. 28:12). That means we have to do our part. That means we have to work. It may be a four-letter word, but there is nothing bad about it.

In fact, work is something God came up with. He says in Matthew 6 that we are not to worry about getting our needs met. We are to look at the birds and see how God provides for them. (Matt. 6:25,26.) Have you ever noticed that worms don't fall from the sky and drop into a birds' mouths while they are just sitting there? No. Those birds get out there and gather up those worms and chow down. God provides the worms, but they have to go get them.

> Therefore take up the whole armor of God, that you may be able to withstand in the evil day, and having done all, to stand.
>
> EPHESIANS 6:13

Many people misunderstand this Scripture. When you ask them what they are doing about their situation, they say, "Well, I'm just standing." And that is all they are doing. They're standing there while their dream is sitting on the shelf. They don't understand that before you can stand, you have to have done all you can to stand.

Have you gone through every avenue available to accomplish your dream? Have you done all that is in your power and ability to accomplish the vision on the inside of you? Only then are you able to say, "Having done all, I am going to stand." There are things that we have to do to fulfill what God has placed in our heart.

Confusion

If something happens that we don't understand, or if things don't turn out the way we think they should, we can get upset and want to just throw in the towel. "Well, it's just not working!" If we cannot understand it, we quit.

Then again, sometimes we are just not sure which way to go. This is why many people will sit there and do nothing. But that's not what the apostle Paul did. Look at Acts 16:6-7. "Now when they had gone through Phrygia and the region of Galatia, they were forbidden by the Holy Spirit to preach the Word in Asia. After they had come down to Mysia, they tried to go to Bithynia, but the Spirit did not permit them."

Paul keeps doing what he knows God has called him to do. God has called him to preach the Word. He has called him to get the good news out to as many people as will listen. Even when he hits a roadblock, he keeps preaching, planting churches, and ministering. He keeps moving.

Paul wrote a majority of the New Testament. He has credentials. He is a man of God determined to do all the will of God in his life. When he starts out for Asia, the Spirit of God forbids him. *No, don't go there.* Many times the Holy Spirit will tell you what not to do, just as much as He will tell you what to do.

When Paul gets this from the Holy Spirit, he listens. "Okay, we are not going there. Well, let's go to Bithynia then." So he heads for Bithynia. The Spirit will not let him go there either. So he just keeps moving.

"So passing by Mysia, they came down to Troas. And a vision appeared to Paul in the night. A man of Macedonia stood and pleaded with him, saying, 'Come over to Macedonia and help us.' Now after he had seen the vision, immediately we sought to go to Macedonia, concluding that the Lord had called us to preach the gospel to them" (Acts 16:8-10). The Word says that he went immediately!

It is important to finish what you start, but you can always find a barrier to keep you from moving forward in the plan of God. Some people think they have to see the finger of God writing things out for them in the sky before they will step out. Some people will have a burning bush experience. God will tell them exactly what to do. *Boom!* This is the way, walk ye in it. This is what I've called you to do. Then they let their heads get in the way. They start to wonder, *Was that really God, or was that just me?* The longer they hesitate to fulfill that vision planted in their heart, the more unsure they get, the more they begin to wonder if maybe it was just too much pizza the night before.

Don't fall into that trap. Don't let that confusion set in. When God puts something in your heart, start moving in that direction. Do what Paul did. Move into action immediately.

Some people think, *But God has never spoken to me. He's never told me what I'm supposed to do.* Many times people have heard from God, but they reasoned it away as nothing. God put a desire in their heart, but because it was not a burning bush experience, they dismissed it. Now they are just wandering around, not sure what to do. If that is you, you need to go back to where you first had that desire in you. Go back there and stir that thing up. Go back to God. "What were You talking to me about? What were You dealing with me about? What were You burning in my heart, Lord?"

Then, when you get hold of that thing, don't put it off again. Don't dismiss it. Go for it. Immediately begin to make plans and preparations to fulfill what God has put in your heart. Keep moving in that direction. As you are moving, God will continue to guide you along. If you start to head the wrong way, trust that God is going to steer you the right way just as He did for Paul. He will funnel you in the direction you are supposed to go.

Sometimes we do not know if our desire is from God until we take steps to fulfill it. It might be God, or it might not be. Sometimes you may start to go there, and when you do, you think, *That was cool, but that was not what God has in store for me.* You just know. Unless you start taking that step to find out, you will always wonder.

So do not let confusion keep you from the plan of God.

Condemnation

I have learned not to live in condemnation. If you are always living in condemnation, you cannot move forward. Condemnation weighs us down, takes away our confidence, and keeps us from being effective in the plan of God. The Word of God tells us that we are not to live under the weight of condemnation. "There is therefore now no condemnation to those who are in Christ Jesus, who do not walk according to the flesh, but according to the Spirit. For the law of the Spirit of life in Christ Jesus has made me free from the law of sin and death" (Rom. 8:1,2).

When you were born again, you were set free from the law of sin and death. You became the righteousness of God in Christ. (2 Cor. 5:21.) Sure, we make mistakes after we are saved. Sure, we fall into temptation and mess up. When we fall, we have to get right back up, confess our sin, be forgiven, and go on with what God has for us.

The devil will try to get you to stay down. He will stick his ugly old foot on your neck and tell you how bad you are and how you cannot be saved if you did such and such. He will try to keep you right there in condemnation for as long as he can, because he knows you will never move forward in the plan of God as long as you are there.

However, you need to pull out your sword, which is the Word of God, and send the devil running. You need to remind him and yourself who you are in Christ. You need to say, "That's all under the blood now. That has been forgiven. That has been tossed into the sea of forgetfulness. I am redeemed from the curse. I have been made the righteousness of God in Christ. Now I'm getting up and going forward with all that God has for me."

Then get up and go for the dream. Don't let condemnation hold you back.

Immorality

It's one thing to mess up, and another thing to continue in immorality. All of us make mistakes. We're not perfect. But when we continue in immorality, it's going to become a barrier to our progression. If you are sleeping around, cheating in business, or sinning on a regular basis, you are putting up a roadblock to your success. God wants to bless you. He wants you to succeed. You are blocking the blessings He wants to get to you when you continue in immoral living.

In 1 Timothy 1:19, Paul charges Timothy to keep fighting the good fight of faith, to keep moving forward in his gifts and his calling. He tells him in verse 19 to have "faith and a good conscience, which some having rejected, concerning the faith have suffered shipwreck." Then, in verse 20, he mentions two people by name: Hymenaeus and Alexander. They are examples of believers who suffered shipwreck on their way to their destiny. The reason they suffered shipwreck is that they rejected two things: (1) faith, and (2) a good conscience.

Bible scholars tell us that Alexander had once been a part of Paul's ministry team. He began to head in directions that he knew were not right. I don't believe that he just woke up one day and decided to oppose Paul. That kind of thing usually starts out with a few wrong decisions. You start to get sloppy about ethics. You start to excuse sin. You take a wrong turn here. You move off in another direction over there. Soon, you're way off track, and *Kshhhh!* You are shipwrecked. When this happens, people turn away from their faith. Instead of running to God, they run the other way.

The Bible says that Alexander rejected a good conscience. In other words, he ignored his conscience more and more and chose to give in to immorality. Then he began to deny the faith. This often happens to people who choose to hang on to their sin. You cannot stay in faith and sin at the same time. You have to choose one or the other. God lays this choice before us in Deuteronomy 30:19. "I have set before you life and death, blessing and cursing; therefore choose life."

You cannot serve God and sin at the same time. If you choose to hang on to your sin, then you are going to end up rejecting faith. Often they don't want to give up their lifestyle, and, therefore, they forfeit the blessings of God. Their prayers do not work. There is a barrier between them and God. It is called the barrier of sin. Then, because they are already so deep into deception, they think, *This faith stuff just doesn't work!* So they reject it. Then their God-given dream suffers shipwreck.

I do not want to suffer shipwreck. If you have suffered shipwreck in your faith, you can get back on course again. God is well able to repair your ship and get you back on track. All it takes is a repentant heart. All it takes is your willingness to turn around and go God's way again.

Just as the father ran to receive the prodigal son, your heavenly Father is ready to run out to meet you on your way back, wrap you in the robe of His righteousness, put that covenant ring back on your finger, and celebrate your destiny with you. God can do some very big things in a short span of time. Don't make Him wait any longer. Choose life and blessing today.

Pride

Pride will block the blessings of God. You can be trucking along at a great pace, fulfilling your destiny, doing the works of God, seeing miracles, and all this stuff. Suddenly, pride sneaks in the back door, and, before you realize what's going on, you are way off track. When you are moving in pride, you are on your own. Things aren't so easy when you are on your own.

When we think that we have to accomplish something all by ourselves, we lose something very important: the effectiveness of teamwork. We have to remember that we are in this whole thing together. Something happens when we work together for the kingdom. We can do far more together than we can apart.

There is one minister I know who became a lone ranger once his ministry started growing. I love this man. He is a great man. However, I noticed that, as his ministry began to take off, he isolated himself. He did not want to let people come in and be a part of his team. He thought everyone was out to get him and was afraid to hire other ministers. He was afraid to get involved with others in the kingdom. In addition, everything was about what he had accomplished. He had worked hard. He had built this ministry. It was what we call the "I syndrome." I did this. I did that. I, I, I. And now there he is, all by himself.

We can accomplish so much more for God when we are willing to link up with others. We need to stay kingdom-minded. Don't isolate yourself. Don't think you can do it alone. If you are going to do great things for God, it's going to take more than just you to do it. It takes us together doing something for the kingdom of God.

I found that out when we put a commercial on MTV. I knew there was no way I could do it by myself. It would take all of us teaming up to do this thing. We raised $100,000 in three months! It was not because one rich person donated it, but because a bunch of sweet little grandmas gave five dollars. Some gave tens, and others gave hundreds of dollars. A man gave three dollars while a teenager gave twenty-five dollars. All this added up because everyone was working together to make it happen. We were able to put a salvation commercial on MTV—something that had never been done before. We can do a lot more together than we can on our own.

Thankfulness will keep you out of pride. Some people have the attitude that everyone owes them. You cannot be grateful with that attitude. That kind of person will not go very far in what God has for him.

In Colossians 3, Paul the apostle gives us some keys to living life more abundantly. He lists several things but then boils it all down in verses 14 and 15. "But above all these things," he says, "put on love, which is the bond of perfection. And let the peace of God rule in your hearts, to which also you were called in one body; and be thankful." Be thankful.

When someone does something for you, do not look at him or her like, "Well, it's about time someone heard from God." If your boss does something nice, do not cross your arms and say, "Well, he owed me that. " That is ungratefulness, which is another word for pride.

Without God and others, our dream cannot be realized. When you begin to see success, thank God. When you see your dream coming true, do not forget who gave you everything to make it happen.

God warns us in Deuteronomy 6:12 that after we are flowing in the blessings, we are not to forget where they came from. "Beware, lest you forget the Lord who brought you out of the land of Egypt, from the house of bondage." Then He goes on to say that if we continue in His Word, it will be well with us. (v. 18.)

If you want to keep progressing in your destiny, you must avoid pride.

Self-Seeking Gain

Dreams crash if you focus only on what you can get for yourself. You won't get far if you are in it only for yourself. You may think you are getting somewhere, but it is a deception. You'll eventually realize that you can get only so far before you either hit a blockade you can't get over, or you have an all-out car wreck.

If all you go after is destiny, you are going to miss it. If all you go after is healing, you are going to miss it. If you will go after God and seek first His kingdom and His righteousness, all these things shall be added to you. (Matt. 6:33.) If you are going to accomplish anything for God, you have to stay kingdom-minded. When you do this—when you reach beyond your own personal gain—that is when you will see God do great things.

Taking Up Offenses

In Luke 17:1, Jesus tells His disciples, "It is impossible that no offenses should come, but woe to him through whom they do come!"

The Greek word for "offense" is *skandalon*.[1] It is where the English word *scandal* comes from. The Greek word skandalon originally referred to the spring that holds the bait on an animal trap. So, when an animal goes for the bait, *boom!* It is trapped. The devil is always trying to get us to grab hold of some bait he sets out on that skandalon of his. He knows that all we have to do is touch that bait, and *boom!* He has us in his snare! He will bait us with all kinds of temptations to take up offense.

Maybe someone said something the wrong way to you or someone did not acknowledge you for something you did. There is the bait. But look out! The minute you grab hold of that offense, *boom!* The trap door slams shut!

And there you are alone with that offense, just staring through the bars as your destiny waits motionless.

Jesus told us that it is impossible to live in this world and not have an opportunity to be offended. The devil will see to it that you have plenty of opportunities. An offense will hold you captive and prevent you from moving forward in effectiveness. It will lock you up so that your gifts cannot be freely released. God doesn't want your effectiveness to be paralyzed. He wants you released to experience the fullness of the destiny He has for you.

I once heard a man of God say that there are two things you need in order to be effective and successful in ministry. Number one, you have to be quick to forgive. Number two, you have to be quick to repent. I believe if we will do those two things, it will keep us pliable. Many times the enemy will come along and try to nip your ministry in the bud and prevent you from achieving what God has for you to do by throwing that old skandalon out there. He will throw that big old beefy thing out there and make you want to sink your teeth into that offense. And the second you do, *spprrngg!!* He has you pinned in that trap, paralyzed from fulfilling the plan of God.

We're told in 2 Timothy 2:24 that "a servant of the Lord must not quarrel." (The King James Version says a servant is not to strive.) It goes on to say, "but be gentle to all, able to teach, patient, in humility correcting those who are in opposition, if God perhaps will grant them repentance, so that they may know the truth, and that they may come to their senses and escape the snare of the devil, having been taken captive by him to do his will" (2 Tim. 2:24-26).

If the devil can get you to grab hold of that skandalon—that offense—and pick it up; he has taken you captive. Hey, I didn't say that. That's what the Bible tells us!

Verse 26 tells us what we can do to "escape the snare of the devil." It says that if they will just "come to their senses," they can escape the devil's snare. When you are chewing on that skandalon, you don't even know that you are in that stinking cage. You are too busy chowing down to realize that you have been taken captive. If someone comes near you, you snarl at them as you are chomping on that offense. You are in that cage, you are miserable, and you are going to make everyone around you miserable too! Then, all of a sudden, that misery might cause you to come to your senses.

That is what happened to the prodigal son in Luke 15. After he runs off to live recklessly in the world and spends everything his dad gave him, he literally winds up in a pigpen. Then, one day he looks at the pods the pigs are eating, and they look good to him. You know that when poopy pig pods start looking good, you are in trouble. So, the Bible says that all of a sudden he came to his senses. (Luke 15:17.) He woke up and smelled the pigs!

When we realize we are in a mess, we should get up and do something about it. Don't wait until it gets so bad you cannot stand it anymore. Do not let it get that far. We need to redeem the time because the days are evil. (Eph. 5:16.) When we see the bait in front of us—when we are walking right toward that offense trap—we need to come to our senses, see that thing for what it is, and walk right past that ugly old trap. We need to pay attention to what's going on, recognize that grabbing hold of an offense is going to get us into trouble, and choose not to take it up.

Notice 2 Timothy 2:26 says that when we are taken captive by the devil, we will do his will. When you hang on to offenses, the devil has you right in the palm of his hand. He has you where he can whisper all kinds of junk into your ear and convince you to feed that offense until it burns a hole in you. He will try to get you to focus on that thing, to nurse it, to talk about it, to center all your thoughts on that. The more you look at that thing, the tighter its grip on you. It will mess up your relationships, ministry, and the plan of God for your life, because you are held captive by it.

I want to stay free! I want to walk in the liberty of God's will. I want to stay free from offenses. I don't have time to be caged up in the devil's trap. I have too much work to do for the kingdom of God! How about you?

In other Scriptures, the word *offense* is also translated from the Greek word *proskomma,* which Vine's Expository Dictionary defines as "an obstacle against which one may dash his foot."[1] In other words, an offense is an obstacle. Holding on to an offense will trip you up and pull you off course.

I know people can abuse others. People can be mean. Then again, at other times, people can get offended at the smallest things. Sometimes the person who offended them doesn't even know he did anything wrong. It all depends on the perspective. Situations can be blown out of proportion. Maybe someone said something that came out in a way that miffed you. Many times people pick up an offense because of their own insecurities. But the thing is this: whether it was something someone did to you on purpose or not, and whether it was a big thing or a little thing, you have to come to your senses and realize that it's not worth picking up. None of it makes any difference when it comes to what it does to you. Most of the time when we hold on to an offense, we are the ones who really suffer over it. We are the ones who get the ulcer over it. We are the ones who ruin our other relationships over it. We are the ones it eats away at. Most of the time, that person who offended you has not even thought about it since. They are carrying on with their life while you are still stuck in that skandalon.

It does not matter whether you think you have "the right" to hang on to some offense. It does not matter what happened or how bad it was. You do not have to grab hold of that offense! You do not have to even pause to look at it. Just walk right past it. Keep moving in your destiny. Keep accomplishing your dream. Don't let any offense hold you captive. God has something better for you than that. He doesn't want you to hang on to that skandalon. Turn loose of that thing and move on. You are responsible for your own actions, and that includes reactions. Don't waste your time with offenses that come up. Go on with what God has for you. Come to your senses. Choose to be a victor rather than a victim.

Psalm 119:165 KJV says, "Great peace have they which love thy law: and nothing shall offend them." Do you know that we can actually walk through life without allowing anything to give us offense? You may think this is not possible, but if it were not possible, the Bible wouldn't have said it is. When you love God's Word and make that Word first, you don't need to take up an offense. Praise God! If you do, get rid of it as quickly as possible. Be quick to forgive, because, when you pick up an offense, you are blocking the flow of the Holy Spirit. That is not something you want to do if you want to move in your destiny.

Disobedience

In some cases, we can put up a roadblock to fulfilling our dream, not by purposely living in immorality, but by failing to do what God has told us to do. Isaiah 1:19 says, "If you are willing and obedient, you shall eat the good of the land; but if you refuse and rebel, you shall be devoured by the sword." Sometimes God will tell someone to do something, but, for one reason or another, they never do it. They don't believe God will provide a way for them to do it, or they just never get around to it. There are always more important things to do first. Whatever their reason, their disobedience becomes a barrier to their progress.

Don't let disobedience keep you from the promises of God. Know that when you choose obedience, it will be well with you. The Israelites knew this when they said, "Whether it is pleasing or displeasing, we will obey the voice of the Lord our God...that it may be well with us" (Jer. 42:6.) God wants it to be well with you. Don't let disobedience keep that from you.

Doing Dumb Stuff

Sometimes we do not get there just because we do dumb stuff. One time, when I was driving out of the parking lot from the airport in Tampa, Florida, I had to get through a toll booth to get home. When I got there, I realized that I didn't have any money for the toll. All I had on me was the check I had gotten for preaching. So I told the lady at the tollbooth that I did not have any cash with me and asked if they could bill me.

"Do you have a credit card?" she asked me.

"Well, no." At that time, my wife would not allow me to carry a credit card, because I was dangerous with a credit card.

"Well, there's a cash machine on the third floor," she told me. "Why don't you go up there, get some cash, and come back?"

"Okay." So I started backing the car up. As I was going backwards around this toll booth, I thought, *This might not be very safe.* You know how you just get that feeling. NO! DON'T DO IT! DANGER! DANGER! I thought, *Man, someone could just come flying around that corner....* It was about two in the morning, and I was tired. I just wanted to get home. So I thought, *Well, what can I do?* So, rather than go back to the tollbooth and tell the lady there that I didn't feel right about driving backwards, guess what I did? I saw the curb there and thought, *Well, I will just jump over that curb in my car, go back around to the cash machine, and come back the right way.* I jumped the curb.

Little did I realize that there were all these closed circuit televisions all over the place. So, as soon as I jumped the curb, all of a sudden, *Wooh, wooh, woohh!* Sirens are going off, blue lights are flashing, and I see airport security flying around the corner toward me. Five security cars pulled up, flung their doors open, and, before I knew what hit me, a guard hops out and points his gun at me. "Freeze right there!"

And I'm just like, "Whoa! Don't shoot!"

"Get out of the car!" he told me.

I got out and stuck my hands in the air. They ran over to me, pinned my head up against the door, made me spread my legs out, and started frisking me. Cars are driving by, watching this whole thing. These men have their guns pulled, lights are flashing, and all these security cars have me sandwiched in. They frisked me, asked me a hundred and one questions, and cussed me up one side and down the other. I am thinking about the "I love Jesus" bumper sticker on the back of my car. Have you ever felt like a disgrace to the kingdom of God?

So then they confiscated everything I had on me, pulled my wallet out, and started flipping through it. Well, then they found my ordination card in there. If things were not hot before, they came alive right then. "A preacher, huh?"

They took me to this little room and started interrogating me. I felt like I was a goner then. I mean, they've got this little light shining on me, and they're all over me. I am thinking, *This is it! I am going to die! I am going to the electric chair for curb jumping!* I am freaking out. I don't know what to do. I pictured the security guards who had been sitting around through the night watch, bored out of their gourds. They see a curb jumper. "Get 'em, boys! Get the K-9 unit! He's a curb-jumper!" I don't know what is going to happen next.

They let me go when they realized I was not a mass murderer. The next morning, when my dad called me, I told him what had happened. "Son," he told me. "That's the devil. That is persecution! That's just an unadulterated attack from the devil!"

That wasn't the devil. That was just me jumping a curb. That was me doing something dumb.

I know there are times when attacks come, but we need to be careful not to blame the devil for our own mistakes. Thank God for forgiveness. Thank God for grace. Right in the middle of the mess we caused, He will forgive us. He will get us turned around and heading in the right direction again.

We have to take responsibility for what we do. When we blow it, we have to admit that we blew it. We may mess up, but when we do, all we have to do is repent, get up, and continue on the path God has for us.

When Other People Block Our Path

Sometimes other people can try to get us to take a detour from our destiny. They will try to get you to do something they think you should be doing. Sometimes even those with the best intentions can stand in our way or cause us to become sidetracked from our dreams. You must be careful with whom you share your God-given dreams. Sometimes even family members can discourage you from fulfilling what God has for you. They see all your shortcomings and say, "Man, you can't even take out the trash or make your bed. What makes you think you can do this?" It is not that they want to see you fail, but they cannot imagine you doing anything that big. They will tell you all the reasons why you cannot do it. That is when you need to find some "can" people to hang out with. You need to find people who will agree that you can do all things through Christ who strengthens you. (Phil. 4:13.) If you keep hanging out with the "can'ts," you are going to get discouraged.

Some people choose to hang around others who belittle them, mock their dreams, and make fun of what they want to do. That will kill your dream. If you are hanging around people who tear you down, get away from them. Find some encouragers and start hanging around them. Don't let discouragers block the plan of God for your life.

Worry Over What Others Think

If you spend too much time worrying about whether someone else is going to approve of you, you are going to lose your focus. If you want to move ahead toward your destiny, you need to stop trying to be a people-pleaser, and decide to be a God-pleaser.

Get Back on Course

Don't let detours or roadblocks keep you from pursuing your dream. If you stumble or fall down, don't stay down. Get back up. Keep pursuing the dream God has put in your heart. Know that God will make a way for you and your dream. Get past the hurdles, and go for the gold!

Chapter 12

Possessing Your Life Dream

But a hireling, he who is not the shepherd, one who does not own the sheep, sees the wolf coming and leaves the sheep and flees; and the wolf catches the sheep and scatters them. The hireling flees because he is a hireling and does not care about the sheep.

JOHN 10:12,13

Being an Owner vs. a Hireling

Owning something makes us care for it better than if we are just renting or borrowing it. When we know it is ours, it means more to us. When we take possession of something, our attitude changes. We take better care of things that are ours.

That is how God wants us to be about the dream He has given us. We need to get rid of the hireling mentality and grab hold of the possession mentality. It's not another job. It is your destiny. It is your calling. It belongs to you. It is important not to mimic someone else's calling. Find what is yours, lay hold of it, and run with it. You are not going to run far with what belongs to someone else.

There is something about ownership that changes a person's attitude toward that thing.

One time when we rented a convention center for a crusade, there was a man there who was supposed to help us with the lights and the setup. But while the rest of us are running all over the place trying to get everything set up in time, this man's just sitting in a chair eating a big hoagie sandwich. He has this greasy T-shirt on, and the sauce from his hoagie is running down the side of his face. I said to him, "Hey, could you help us? We are about to start in just a few minutes, and we really need your help. Could you grab that thing and run those wires over there please?"

He just sat there. "Can't do it," he said.

"Why not?"

"Union. Can't do it." He keeps eating his sandwich.

"What do you mean?" I asked him.

"Can't do it, man. I would be fired. Union. My job is to open the curtain. That is it. That's my job."

It was just a job to him. He was not in the union; the union was in him. I thought, *How boring and miserable that must be. Why would you even want to get out of bed in the morning just to open and close some curtain?*

Now, if that had been his calling, he would have been excited about it. "Oh, boy! I get to open and close that curtain! I am ready. Yes!" It is not drudgery when you know it is yours. There is a huge difference between going through the motions and moving in your destiny.

Years ago they tried something in the car manufacturing business to improve the quality of the work. They started putting the first and last names of the assembly line workers on the parts they were responsible for. If a man were in charge of putting the fender on a car, he would get his name on that fender. Well, the quality of car manufacturing went way up after that because it wasn't just any old fender. It was his fender. It had his name on it, so he wanted to make sure it was on there right. No more slamming that thing together, screwing in a few bolts, and thinking, *Well, good enough.* The workers started taking pride in what they were doing.

They wanted to make sure their part fit exactly right and looked great because that thing belonged to them.

Lay Hold of What Belongs to You

I press on, that I may lay hold of that for which Christ Jesus has also laid hold of me.

PHILIPPIANS 3:12

The words "lay hold of" here literally mean "to seize, to take possession of."[2] Paul is talking about pressing on into his destiny. The thing "for which Christ Jesus has also laid hold of" is his calling. In other words, God has grabbed hold of Paul and burned that thing into his spirit. In verse 14, he says, "I press toward the goal for the prize of the upward call of God in Christ Jesus." But, in case we assume that he's referring only to his own calling, he says in the next verse, "Therefore let us, as many as are mature, have this mind" (v. 15).

Your dream belongs to you, and it is up to you to fulfill it. It is not up to your mom or dad to make it happen. It is not up to your spouse to make it happen. It is not up to your pastor or anyone else. It is up to you because it belongs to you. You have to take care of it.

In Hebrews 10:23, we are told to "hold fast" to the confession of our hope without wavering. In Greek, the term "hold fast" has a very similar meaning to "lay hold of" in Philippians 3:12. "Lay hold of" literally means to grab hold of something you have been searching for all your life. You are looking and suddenly find it. You grab hold of that thing and hang on to it with the fierce determination of a bulldog that's never going to let go of what is his. No man, no woman, no circumstance, no devil, no windstorm is going to get it. Why? Because it is yours! That is what it means to "hold fast."

Possess What You Do

Many people think of their vocation as a job. "Well, I'm just a welder." There are those who carry that same attitude into whatever they are doing in ministry. "Well, bless God, I'm just a minister." You need to get past that just-a-job mentality. If all you have is a job, it is time to start moving into your destiny.

I am not saying you should quit your job right away. I have already stressed how important it is to be faithful where you are. However, if you're putting in time somewhere for years and years just to have a job, that's time and energy that could be invested in the destiny God has called you to.

When you step into your destiny, there is nothing else like it. It is not something you do just to get by. It is what you are. It is a part of you. You meditate on it. You go to bed with that thing still in your heart. I cannot tell you how many times I go to bed at night and see myself preaching. I see myself giving altar calls. I see people getting born again. I see myself laying hands on people and they are healed. I see lives being touched by the power of God. I see the Spirit of God moving, because that is my destiny. That is what God has put in my heart. I have taken hold of it. It is mine. It belongs to me.

I know people who are carpenters, and, man, they love what they are doing. They love building more than anything else. They cannot under-stand why anyone would ever want to do anything else but carpentry, because that is their destiny. It is their passion. It is what God has put in their hearts to do.

It does not matter if you are called to be an electrician, a carpenter, a plumber, a doctor, a chef, a secretary, or whatever. The important thing is that you are doing what God has called you to do.

If you don't love what you are doing, you need to do one of two things: either change your attitude, or find something that you love to do and never work another day in your life! When you are doing what you are called to do, it doesn't seem like work to you. When I preach, I have such a blast! I don't call that work. I call that having fun!

One time, after I had given a motivational talk to a group of teachers at a university, this lady grabbed me on the way out. "My goodness!" she said. "I have never seen anyone enjoy what he does as much as you do!" That was a wonderful compliment for me. It is also the truth.

I remember before we started pastoring Destiny Church, I was out there preaching to everything that moved. I was traveling all over, evangelizing with everything in me. And I loved it because it's what God called me to do at that time. After our daughter, Nicole, was born, the grace for that lifted from my wife. She knew it was time for her to stay home with the children. "This is where I belong," she told me. However, she didn't want to hold me back, so she said, "But honey, you have to go to work. I know you love what you do, and...." Then she started crying. That is because the grace had lifted for me as well.

Ever since we started pastoring this church, I have never once heard her say, "Well, I guess you'd better go to church. We've gotta get over there tonight." No. We are excited to go to church. Why is that? It is because God has given us grace to do what we are doing now. We are moving in the call of God.

It is important to follow the grace of God. When I was supposed to be on the road, we both had God's grace to do that. When it was time to begin a new season in our ministry, God's grace moved from the call to evangelism to the call to pastor a church.

We have to learn to go beyond just doing what we do. We have to possess what we do. When we do that, not only will it be a major blessing to others, but it will be a major blessing to us.

Paul did not get out there and say, "Well, I guess I'd better do some preaching. I hope a few get saved tonight." No. He had a passion for what he did. He knew his purpose and he fulfilled it with zeal. Look at what he says in Romans 9:3. I like how it reads in the New Living Translation. "For my people, my Jewish brothers and sisters. I would be willing to be forever cursed—to be cut off from Christ—if that would save them."

That is what happens when you take possession of the dream God has called you to fulfill.

Moses had this same kind of zeal for those he was called to minister to. After the children of Israel had blown it big time, Moses went to God and said, "Oh, these people have sinned a great sin, and have made for themselves a god of gold! Yet now, if You will forgive their sin—but if not, I pray, blot me out of Your book which You have written" (Ex. 32:31,32). That is giving all of yourself over to that calling. That is making it yours. That's caring about what belongs to you. That is possessing your life dream.

Ownership Means Responsibility

When you know something is yours, you take responsibility for it. You understand that you are the one who has to take care of it. You are the one who has to see that it is done right. If something goes wrong, you take responsibility for it. You do not say, "Well, that's not my job." No. You just take care of it.

I learned something very valuable when I first started doing a television program called "Fire By Night." I had never done anything on television at the time, so I did not know which end of a camera to look into. I had to write sketches when I had never done a sketch in my life. I read books and learned as I was doing it. As I was working at it and trying to do the best I could, a young man named Rodney came up to me and said, "Eastman, you're doing really great. It is exciting to see. But there is one thing you need to do. You need to possess "Fire By Night." This needs to be your baby. It needs to be yours."

When he said that to me, the lights came on. I thought, *That is exactly right. I need to possess this thing. This is mine. This is where God has me, and, if it's going to be done, it's up to me to do it.* I recognized that (1) I needed to take ownership; and (2)ownership meant responsibility. I needed to take care of it and make sure it was growing in the direction it was supposed to.

When I began to do that, the program took off. I made it mine, and that made all the difference. We changed the name to "This Generation," and God gave us amazing favor with it. Now it is doing very well. In fact, it is the number-one rated Christian teen program, reaching millions for the kingdom of God.

If God has put something in your heart to do, possess it. Make it yours. It will make all the difference.

Just because you are doing something for someone else does not mean you cannot make it yours. It may not be your ministry or your company. It may not even be your idea. But, if it is something you are supposed to be doing, you can still possess it and take responsibility for it. That does not mean that you should try to take over the company or anything like that. Submit to the one you are working under and respect his or her authority. Take responsibility for what you have been given to do.

There is a man who works with the youth in our church who did this at his job. He went there after hours to clean up the place and make sure everything was all set up and ready for the next day. No one told him he had to do that. His boss was not looming over his shoulder telling him he needed to do that or else. No. He did it of his own volition because he had taken ownership of that job. He cares about how things are run there. He cares about the business. He cares that everything is set up just right so things will run smoothly. He has made it his. He's applied the Scripture that says, "And whatever you do, do it heartily, as to the Lord and not to men, knowing that from the Lord you will receive the reward of the inheritance; for you serve the Lord Christ" (Col. 3:23). And Ecclesiastes 9:10 says, "Whatever your hand finds to do, do it with your might." And now, because of the seeds of faithfulness he has sown, he is one of the managers there. Not only that, he has such favor there that they let him take time off to do his crusades and preach Jesus. They do not let anyone else there do that. That is the favor of God. He brings promotion.

If you are going to possess your destiny, you are going to have to turn loose of the other things that occupy your hands. If your hands are filled with all kinds of other activities, you won't have room to grab hold of your destiny. In Hebrews 12:1, we're urged to "lay aside every weight...and let us run with endurance the race that is set before us."

We can't run freely the race set before us if we've got all these other things hanging on to us. These weights might be old habits or hobbies or busy things in your life. They are like parasites. They are the things that hang on and suck all the life out of you. They are the things that hold you down and keep you from being effective. They cling to you and feed off you, rather than your feeding off them. They possess you and keep you from possessing what you are really supposed to be possessing.

Shake them off. Lay them aside. Say goodbye to them so you can say hello to your destiny.

A lady told me after service one day that she has a friend who is living in sin. This friend is a born-again Christian. She knows she is living in sin, but she does not want to let go of that sin. This lady told me that she's tried talking to her friend and telling her that God has something so much better for her than that, but she would just smile and say, "Well, I know that. I'm just like this, and I guess I'll never get better." She didn't want to let go of that sin, although it was keeping her from God's better plan for her. As long as she lets that old parasite keep its hooks in her, she will never take possession of the destiny God has for her.

The Designer Knows

I heard a story about a man who was out driving his new Model T one day when, all of a sudden, it stopped running. So he got out, popped the hood, and started scratching around under there. Since this was when Model T's first came out, he had no idea how to get it running again. He had never even seen an engine before, and he was not very mechanical.

Well, as he was trying to figure out what to do, this huge limousine pulled up beside him and a man in French cuffs stepped out. "Having trouble with your car?" he asked.

"Yeah," the man under the hood said, "it just stopped. Don't know what it is. Won't turn over."

So the man in the French cuffs asked him if he had some tools with him.

"Yeah, sure. They're in the back." At that time, little toolboxes came with the car.

So the man from the limousine got some tools, rolled up his French cuffs, and started tweaking around under the hood. After a little bit, he said, "Get back in the car and try to fire it up."

As soon as the man turned the ignition, *Vrrrrooooom*. It started right up. So the man in the cuffs closed the hood and walked back to his limousine.

"Hey," the other man said. "How'd you do that? What did you do under there? I mean, you don't look like you know anything about cars."

The man in the French cuffs got back into his limousine, stuck his hand out the window, and said, "Hi. My name's Henry Ford. I made the car you are driving. Just thought I'd help out."

The man in the fancy clothes knew how to fix that car because he designed it. It was his invention, his doing. He knew how to make it run right.

God made each one of us. He is the One who knows what is going to fulfill us the most. He's the One who knows what is going to make us happiest. He is the One who knows what we are designed to do best. When God first called me into the ministry, I thought God was going to stick me with something I hated to do. I thought I would be shoveling duck manure the rest of my life. I did that for my dad. I cleaned up duck poop. So I really thought, *Well, if I am going to do things right, I will be shoveling this stuff up the rest of my life.* I was willing to do that, but that is not what God called me to do.

God doesn't tell you to do something without first giving you the desire to do it. God dropped a desire into my heart. It was not a desire to shovel duck poop. It was a desire to reach a generation for Jesus and to help people realize their destiny in life. When God calls us to do something, He gives us the desire and the ability to do it.

Chapter 13

Feed Your Dream

God wants your dream to flourish even more than you do. If it is going to flourish, it is going to need some dream feed.

When all kinds of other things in life are competing for our time and attention, it can be tempting to let our dream die on the vine. God doesn't want your dream squashed. He doesn't want it choked off by weeds or eaten up by the enemy. If you want that dream to grow strong, you have to keep feeding it. If you want to thrive rather than just barely survive, you have to pull out the dream feed.

So, how do you do that?

1. Feed Your Dream With the Word of God and Prayer

Keep pouring the promises of God into your heart. Meditate on the Word. Pray the Word. Declare the Word over your dream. The Word of God in your heart will feed the dream God has put there. That dream needs the Word of God to survive. If you try to carry out your purpose without the Word, you are going to run out of steam before you get very far. Don't forget who put the dream in your heart. Don't forget who the Word is to begin with.

2. Give Your Dream Lots of Sunshine

When things start trying to pull you down and you feel yourself getting discouraged, start to think about the goodness of God and what He's done in your life. Think about what He is able to do and what He is still going to do. Think about how He gave you that dream and how God is faithful and true to finish what He starts. Fix your thoughts on whatever is good, true, and right.

When you start to feel overwhelmed and think it can't happen, remember what the Lord says in Mark 10:27: "With men it is impossible, but not with God; for with God all things are possible." It may look impossible for you to do, but that is not what God says. When you do this, it is going to do something to you on the inside. It's going to strengthen the dream in your heart and cause it to shoot up and start bearing fruit.

3. Speak the Right Things Over Your Dream

Proverbs 18:21 says, "Death and life are in the power of the tongue, and those who love it will eat its fruit." Your own tongue can either kill or nourish your dream. Choose to nourish your dream with the right words. When you are tempted to say, "It'll never happen," STOP! Don't say it! Instead, say, "Thank You, Lord, for making my dream a reality. Thank You that with You all things are possible. Thank You that You're the Way-Maker and that You're making a way for my dream right now!"

4. Protect Your Dream

Protect your dream from the naysayers. Protect it from people who will try to shoot down your dream, people who will ridicule you and try to plant doubt in you.

If you want your dream to prosper, you are going to have to protect it.

God called you to flourish. He wants you to flourish in your destiny. Webster's Dictionary defines the word *flourish* in this way: "to blossom; to grow vigorously; succeed; thrive; prosper; to be at the peak of development, activity, influence, production, etc; be in one's prime." This is what God wants for you and your destiny. He wants you to blossom, to grow vigorously, to succeed, thrive, and prosper. He wants to bring you to the peak of your development, activity, production, and influence. God planted that dream in you. He wants you to prosper and succeed so that you can declare the goodness of God.

Proverbs 11:28 says, "The righteous will flourish like foliage." And in verse 30, it says, "The fruit of the righteous is a tree of life, and he who wins souls is wise."

It is God's desire that you flourish in your destiny.

Reach to the Sky

Have you ever noticed how trees, flowers, and plants always reach upward toward the sun? Unless there is something seriously wrong with them, they grow upward. It is as if they are stretching as high as they can to the sky. And that's how they flourish.

God raised you up to be a world-changer. He raised you up to make a difference. However, if you are going to do that, you have to keep looking up. You have to keep your eyes off the circumstances that try to uproot your dream and look up toward God. Get your eyes off all the little mundane attacks. Look up and see the big picture that God has for your life. As you begin to do that, all the oppression, all the guilt, all the condemnation and discouragement is going to fall off you like water off a duck's back.

> "Arise [from the depression and the prostration in which circumstances have kept you—rise to a new life]! Shine (be radiant with the glory of the Lord), for your light has come, and the glory of the Lord has risen upon you."
>
> ISAIAH 60:1 AMP

It is time to rise up to a new life! Shine! Be radiant with the glory of the Lord! For your light has come and the glory of the Lord is risen upon you. It is your time to blossom, grow, and bear fruit for the Lord. So get up out of the depression. Get up out of the discouragement. Get up out of all those attacks the devil may throw at you to hold you down. This is your time and this is your place, because this is where God has planted you now. Don't wait for tomorrow. Rise up today, take your place, and move in the direction that God is calling you. As you do, you will thrive and bear much fruit.

The more you grow in the things of God, the more you start thinking and feeling the way God does and the more you want to help people and do everything you can to minister. I noticed the closer I started growing to the Lord, the more I wanted God to touch our family, schools, and city. As I continued to grow, the more the vision expanded and grew. Soon my heart's desire went beyond just my city into the whole region I was in. Then it went beyond my region to my state; then beyond that to the nation. And now my vision is to reach the whole world. That is what happens when you feed your dream. The passion of God begins to grow in you. A passion to reach the world rises in you. You are no longer content to just sit there doing the minimum to get by because God's desires are pushing up into your heart. The more you feed those desires, the bigger they get because God is a big God, and He believes in giving us big dreams and big blessings and big passions.

He is El Shaddai, the God of more than enough. He likes to inundate us with more and more of Him and His goodness. It is His nature, and He wants us to be like Him. And the more we become like Him, the bigger we're going to dream, the more we're going to feed those dreams, and the more fruit we're going to bear.

Now is the time for you to thrive in the dream God has given you to fulfill. Now is the time for you to move beyond just surviving and begin thriving. God wants to prosper you and give you good success. He wants to grow your dream and bless all the work of your hand. He has so much for you. If you are going to flourish in your destiny, you have to keep feeding the dream.

Chapter 14

Hold Fast to Your Life Dream

Let us hold fast the confession of our hope without wavering, for
He who promised is faithful.

HEBREWS 10:23

Hold fast to the dream God gives you. You need to hang on to it with
everything in you. When the devil comes along and tries to get you to turn
loose of it, don't do it. When storms come and try to bowl you over and
get you to drop that dream, hold fast! Hang on to the promises of God,
and don't let anything or anyone take them away. Know that they belong
to you. God put the dream in your heart, not to lay aside, but to fulfill.
When people try to talk you into putting it down to pick up something
else, don't you do it. Don't let anyone persuade you to let go of that dream
to do what they think you should do. No. Hold fast to the vision God has
given you; hang on to it with everything in you.

Have you ever seen little kids who find something they really want? What
do they do? They grab hold of that thing and clamp their little fists around
it with unbelievable determination. Sometimes it amazes me how much
strength the little guys have when they have their fist around something
they really want. If you are going to get it out of their hand, you have to
work hard to pry that thing loose. Now, granted, most of the time they are
not mature enough to know the difference between what's good and what's
bad for them. But you have to admire the strength of their determination.
What made them grab hold of that thing to begin with? They wanted it.

Once they had it in their hand, they were determined not to let anyone take it from them.

That is how we need to be with the dream God gives us. We have to desire it. We have to want it. And once we've got hold of it—once we've possessed it as ours—we've got to be determined to never let anything or anyone take it from us.

That is how Bartimaeus was.

> Now they came to Jericho. As He went out of Jericho with His disciples and a great multitude, blind Bartimaeus, the son of Timaeus, sat by the road begging. And when he heard that it was Jesus of Nazareth, he began to cry out and say, "Jesus, Son of David, have mercy on me!" Then many warned him to be quiet; but he cried out all the more, "Son of David, have mercy on me!" So Jesus stood still and commanded him to be called. Then they called the blind man, saying to him, "Be of good cheer. Rise, He is calling you." And throwing aside his garment, he rose and came to Jesus. So Jesus answered and said to him, "What do you want Me to do for you?" The blind man said to Him, "Rabboni, that I may receive my sight." Then Jesus said to him, "Go your way; your faith has made you well." And immediately he received his sight and followed Jesus on the road.
>
> MARK 10:46-52

Bartimaeus was not about to let anyone keep him from what he wanted. He did not like where he was (blind and poor), and he was determined to get Jesus' attention so he would be healed. So he cried out with everything in him, "Jesus! Son of David! Have mercy on me!" All the people around him were trying to shut him up. "Shh! Hush! Don't bother Him. You're making a scene." Bartimaeus cried all the louder, "Jesus! Have mercy on me!" Everyone still tried to keep him quiet, but he refused to listen. He refused to give up. He was going to get his healing, and that was that! That is tenacity. If you want something bad enough, you have to be tenacious. You have to hold fast to that with all your strength and determination. You have to get stubborn about it.

There will be people in your life who will try to shut you up when you start talking about your dream. They will try to get you to quiet down about Jesus and His plan. "Shh. Hush. Don't get so excited. Don't get charismatic on us now. This isn't the place for that. Be quiet."

They will try to get you back into religion. They will try to rob you of your passion. They will try to stifle your zeal for God. And the devil will try to get you to keep quiet. He will try to get you to sit back down and act like a beggar again. That is when you need to rise and cry out to God even more! That is when you need to be like Bartimaeus and shout, "God has more for me than this! God has a destiny for me! He has a future and a hope for me! He has plans for me! He has plans for health and prosperity and success! He has the fulfillment of my heart's dream! I am a winner, not a loser! I will never accept defeat! I will never quit! I will never let go of the destiny God has for me!"

Bartimaeus knew that God had something more for him than just sitting on the side of the road, blind and begging. He knew that God had a destiny for him. He knew that God had health and healing for him. He knew there was something more he had to do with his life besides just sitting there letting the devil run over him every day. He knew that he needed healing if he was going to accomplish God's purpose for him. So he cried out with stubborn determination to lay hold of what God had for him.

The minute Jesus called to him, he stood up, flung aside his beggar's coat, and ran to Jesus. Now, when you study up on that beggar's garment, you will learn that it was what gave him the license to be a beggar. It labeled him and gave him the right to accept alms. It was sort of like a uniform with a little nametag. When he stood up and flung that garment aside, he made a strong statement. He was saying, "I'm not going to need this anymore. No longer will I live the life of a begger. I am going from where I am to a better place. And I'm not going to need that where I'm going!"

Then, when he gets to Jesus, Jesus asks him a question that seems a little ridiculous on the surface. "Bartimaeus," He asks him, "What can I do for you?" The man's blind, right? Jesus knows he is blind. Everyone knows he is blind. Jesus wants to know what's in his heart. He wants to know where his desire is. He wants to know what his passion is. "What do you want Me to do for you, Bartimaeus? What is the dream you have got burning on the inside of you? What is it you want?"

"I want to see," Bartimaeus tells him.

So Jesus smiles and says, "According to your faith be it given to you." *Bam!* He is healed instantly. He can see clearly. He has vision. He has purpose. He got up and moved to a better place because he was determined not to settle for less.

That is how you need to be when it comes to your destiny. Do not settle for less than what you know God has for you. Do not let anyone talk you into accepting less. Be tenacious. Be persistent.

If you hit a bump in the road, do not automatically accept it and say, "Well, I guess it just wasn't meant to be." Stay tenacious.

Maybe God spoke to you and told you to be a part of a particular organization, but, when you applied for the job, nothing happened. Well, turn in your resumé again. If nothing happens, turn it in again! Don't quit. You do not need to be rude. You don't need to be a pest. Just smile and say, "I'm going to be the best employee you've ever had. All you've got to do is sign me on, then watch what I'm going to do for you." Believe God for that job. As you believe God, keep on doing something. Keep on applying. Keep on knocking.

"Seek, and ye shall find; knock, and it shall be opened unto you" (Matt. 7:7 KJV). I like the Amplified Version: "Keep on asking and it will be given you; keep on seeking and you will find; keep on knocking [reverently] and [the door] will be opened to you."

If you know in your heart that God has called you to do something, don't take no for an answer. Keep on keeping on. Keep heading the direction you know God has called you in. There is power in tenacity.

Never Give Up

Many times people will get all fired up when God first drops a dream into their heart. They know that God has something special for them to do. Something happened: a spark went off on the inside of them and there's an explosion. Then a day goes by. A week goes by, a month, a year, and then a decade. They still have not seen the fulfillment of that dream. They become discouraged. They lose persistence. That fiery edge begins to fade, and they think, *Well, I guess it's never going to come to pass.* Soon, they stop or take a detour. They try to do something different. They begin to settle for mediocrity.

Sometimes I hear people say things like, "Well, if you're in the will of God, everything's just gonna happen naturally. It will be like walking up to the electric doors at the grocery store. You just step up and the doors open." That is not how it is. Stuff happens. Hindrances come. Situations will come against you. The devil will try to block your way. People will try to get you to do other things. Sometimes life just gets in the way. Sometimes it is not God's timing. We talked about all that earlier. Many times, when the vision doesn't come to pass right away, people get discouraged and give up.

You need to keep that dream stirred up even if it is not happening when you would like it to. I remember before we got on TV, people would come up to me and ask me what I wanted to do. "I want to get on TV. I want to reach the world for Jesus. I want to change a generation."

A few weeks later, they would come back and say, "I thought you were doing that TV thing."

"I am!"

"Well, where is it?"

"Well, it's not my time yet. I have an appointed time. It's not my time yet, but it's coming."

What was I doing? I was maintaining the zeal. I was keeping the fire burning. That is what you have to do. Do not let the fire go out just because circumstances get in the way. Do not give up just because it does not happen right away. Know that it is coming. Keep pressing on in faith, and God will bring it to pass.

Look at what Paul says in 2 Corinthians 1:8-10:

> "For we do not want you to be ignorant, brethren of our trouble which came to us in Asia: that we were burdened beyond measure, above strength, so that we despaired even of life. Yes, we had the sentence of death in ourselves, that we should not trust in ourselves but in God who raises the dead, who delivered us from so great a death, and does deliver us; in whom we trust that He will still deliver us."

I like that. That is how we need to talk. Remind yourself, *God delivered me from bad circumstances in the past, He is delivering me now, and He is going to deliver me in the future.*

When tough times come, do not camp there in the middle of trouble. Keep on going through.

Just Keep Going

A good friend and I were scheduled to minister at a juvenile delinquent center. We were to arrive at 10:00 P.M., so we headed out together about 8:00. I had been there before, so I knew where to go. I had been in there, in fact, before I was born again. This time, I was going to go back there with guns blazing. We were driving down the road, singing songs, praising God, and praying all the way. We were ripping in tongues, and we were excited. Suddenly, it got foggy. It was so thick that we could not see where we were going. So we slowed down to about twenty miles an hour. We are just chick, chick, chicking along when I noticed all these other cars whizzing right by. *Whoosh! Whoosh!* I mean, they are just flying past us at seventy-five and eighty miles an hour. I thought, *How are they seeing? We can't even see out the window.*

Well, all of a sudden, a revelation hit me. Wipe the window. Duh. So I took my hand and wiped the window. Man! It was condensation on the inside—not fog! I thought we had worked ourselves into such a frenzy praising God in that car that it fogged up all the windows! But that was not it. Sorry. What had happened was that something went wrong with the defroster. All this steam was pouring out the defroster vent, and that is what was fogging up the windows. (This was before my friend understood that God has the best for us, you understand. So he had this old, beat up car at that time.) We tried shutting the defroster off. As soon as we shut it off, it started spewing hot water. We did not know what was going on. A mechanic could probably tell you what was happening, but all we knew was that something weird was going on and we could not see.

It never even occurred to us to stop, turn around, and go back. No, we knew we had something to do, and we were not going to let some goofy little car problem stop us. Well, when the little lights came on and started flashing some kind of warning—I think it said something about being overheated—we pulled into a gas station. While I put some water in the car, my friend went to telephone the center for directions. When he got back, he looked shocked.

"What's wrong?" I asked.

"They told me that they don't have us scheduled for tonight. They don't even have a record that we're supposed to be there."

I pulled out my daytimer. "Here, this is who I talked to. Here is the time I talked to him. Go back and call again. Give them his name."

So, after he tried again, he hollered at me from the phone booth. "Eastman! They still say we can't come!"

I grabbed the telephone and talked to them. "I talked to so-and-so and he said we could come."

"Well, sir, we don't have any record of your being able to come. We can't allow you in this place without permission."

"Well," I said, "we'll keep on going. We'll see you in a little bit then." I hung up the telephone.

"Well, what did they say?" my friend pressed.

I did not tell him what they said. I just looked at him and said, "We're going! Come on!" So we got back in the car and kept driving.

Many people would have bailed out right there. They would say, "Well, they said we can't come. I guess we can't. We had better go back. It just did not work out. The Lord works in mysterious ways."

No! Keep going. If God puts something in your heart, keep running with it.

Well, by the time we finally got there, the man who had booked us had come, so we got in okay. He ran through that place with the exploding hot water bottle and seventy people were born again that night! After I preached, over forty people were baptized in the Holy Spirit. One of them was a jailer. Now, when you have a jailer there with his hands up in the air worshiping God in tongues, you know you have revival!

We could have bailed out halfway there. We could have stopped right when the car started spewing water, or when they said, "We're sorry. You can't come here." That is what many people do. They bail out before they get there. They bail out when things do not go smoothly. Do not do it. Don't give up. Hang on to your vision. Hold fast to what God has put in your heart to do. Keep going. If bad circumstances come, keep plowing right through it. Don't grow weary in well doing, for in due season, you are going to reap because you're not going to faint. (Gal. 6:9.) Say, "I'm not going to give up. I will not faint. I will not accept defeat because I am a winner! I am not a loser. I'm a winner!"

"But resist [the devil], firm in your faith, knowing that the same experiences of suffering are being accomplished by your brethren who are in the world" (1 Peter 5:9 NASB). Sometimes, when we're going through trials, we think we're the only ones who have ever been through anything like it. But we need to remember that there are other people who have gone through tough times, too. They have made it through victoriously. So can you!

In Habakkuk 2:2-3, the Lord talks about the importance of writing our vision down "that he may run who reads it." If you've ever tried running with something in your hand, you know you've got to hang on to that thing so you don't drop it. In verse 3 it says, "The vision is yet for an appointed time; but at the end it will speak, and it will not lie. Though it tarries, wait for it." I looked that word wait up in the Hebrew and discovered that it literally means "to adhere to, to stick to, to cling to." Anyone can obtain a vision for his life, but it takes a person of faith to walk that vision out, to maintain it, and to cling to it. That is what God wants us to do.

I heard someone say, "Christians need to be like postage stamps. They need to stick with it until they get to their destination." God wants us to have that kind of stick-to-it-ness. We have to be willing to stick with it even when the going is tough. We have to stick it out when it does not feel good to stick it out. We have to be determined to hold fast to the dream God has given us to the very end.

However, many people bail out in the middle of it. They bail out when it gets a little difficult. They bail out when it is not as much fun as they would prefer. They bail out when the devil beats up on them and tugs at that dream. They give in and let him have it. The Word of God commands us to "wait for it," to adhere to it, to cling to it, and to stick to it like glue. It may seem like it is tarrying. It may seem like it is taking a long time. But "wait for it; because it will surely come" (Hab. 2:3). When the going gets tough, get tough and hang on to that dream with even more determination. Don't hand it over to the devil. Don't do it! If you will hang on to it and use it for God's glory, God will make a great feast of it to feed the multitudes.

It is going to take faith to hang on to it. The Bible says, "the just shall live by faith" (Rom. 1:17). Faith is not something you pull out when the going gets rough. It's a lifestyle. You do not pop in and out of faith. You live by faith. You walk by faith. You talk by faith. You think by faith. You dream by faith.

The Power of Hope

"Now faith is the substance of things hoped for, the evidence of things not seen" (Heb. 11:1).

When you live a life of faith, it brings substance to your life. It brings substance to your dream. Now, there is something else I want you to see here. It says here that faith is the substance of things hoped for. Hope is a good thing. If you are not careful, you can begin to think that hope is your enemy. Hope is not bad. True, it is not the same thing as faith. Hope is what you stick your faith to. If you don't have hope, you don't have anything to stick your faith to. Hope is a vision of something better than where you are today. It is what you see tomorrow. You have to have hope. If you do not have hope, all you have is hopelessness. We all know that is a bad place to be. If you have ever seen anyone who has lost all hope, it is not a pretty sight. If you have ever felt hopeless, it is no fun at all.

You have to have hope. Some people say, "I don't want to get my hopes up." Yes, you do! Get those hopes up! You cannot have faith if you do not have hope first. Look at Hebrews 11:1 again: "Now faith is the substance of things hoped for." Faith is what gives substance to the things you are hoping for. It is what causes you to see it in the spirit. You see it in faith.

I remember years ago, before my wife and I had Sumner or Nicole, we had believed God for children for eight years. We had done everything we knew to do. We were believing God and hanging on to His promise. We bound and rebuked every devil we could think of. We were standing on our confessions of faith. I mean, we were marching around, shouting, "In the name of Jesus!" Then all of a sudden, we got a revelation what faith is. Faith is where you rest. It is that place where you lean on the Lord. You put your confidence in Him and His ability to take care of it for you. So then, when people would ask us where our kids were, we would say, "They're on the way."

"When?" they would ask.

"They're coming. Praise God!"

We knew that God was taking care of it. We did not have to give it another thought. God was working on it. He knew the desires of our hearts, and He was working on fulfilling them. Ten years ago Sumner was born. We have a daughter, Nicole, too. God is good!

Right after Sumner was born, I hardly let anyone touch him. I had waited for this boy, and I was sure going to hold fast to him now! I was the first man to change his diapers. I bathed him. I held him. I mean, this was my kid! When the grandparents wanted to see him, I would just hold him up so they could have a look. I was not about to let him go. I honestly did not want anyone to hold him. I had to fight with my mother-in-law a couple times over it. I am not kidding. I had waited eight years for that baby, and I was not about to turn loose of him. It took three months for me to even let my wife bathe him—and that was only because I was out of town.

What are you believing God for? What vision has He put in your heart? Whatever it is, do not turn loose of it. Do not give up hope. Do not let the devil steal it away from you. Hold fast to your destiny, and God is going to bring it to pass with power and grace.

Commitment

"Commit your works to the Lord, and your thoughts will be established" (Prov. 16:3). I like the New Living Translation of this verse. "Commit your work to the Lord, and then your plans will succeed." God not only wants us to have plans; He wants us to have successful plans. He wants His plan for us to succeed. He wants us to prosper in our destiny. The Word says that we need to commit our work to the Lord, then our plans will succeed. When we commit to complete the work God has for us to do, God is going to bless that with success. When you know what God has called you to do, commit that to Him. Then do it with all your heart, soul, and strength. That is when God moves in and starts on the miracles you need.

When you commit to something, you hold fast to it. You cannot let it slip away. You don't push it to the side. You do not allow it to become lost in all the piles of paper on your desk. No. You are committed to doing it. It does not matter if it is convenient or not. It does not matter if it is easy or not.

It does not matter if something else comes up that is more appealing. If you have committed to do it, you are going to do it. That is how you need to be when it comes to accomplishing your dream. You have to stay committed. Do not get wishy-washy about it. Don't think, *Well, I guess maybe I'll do it if there's nothing better to do or if it's not too complicated.* No. Be a person of integrity. Be a person of commitment. People of commitment finish what they start. They do not begin something then just forget about it. They hold to it. God wants you to be committed to your dream. He wants to depend on you to fulfill it. He has entrusted you with it, but it is your job to commit to it.

Maybe you are reading this and thinking, *But Eastman, I've already let go of my dream. I didn't hold fast to it like I should have. I blew it. Things got hard and there was all this stuff to deal with, so I just dropped the ball.*

It's never too late to pick that dream up again. If you have let it go, don't just sit there thinking it is hopeless. The game's not over. As long as there's breath left in you, it's not too late to go after it again. God's calling is without repentance. (Rom. 11:29.) If you have fallen down, get right back up again. If you have been pulled off course, get back on track again. Don't just sit there on the side of the road and let discouragement and condemnation roll over you like a bulldozer. Get up! Get going! So what if you made some mistakes. Repent and move on.

Ask God to forgive you, forgive yourself, and get back on the path to your destiny. "Yeah, but what if I blow it again?" Okay. You may trip along the way again. You may blow it again. That does not mean that you quit. It does not mean you cannot get right back up again, get clean with God, and move right back into your destiny again. God has a way of making up for lost time, even when we have messed up. He is not looking for perfect people to do His work. He is looking for willing people. He is looking for people who realize they cannot do it by themselves, that they do need God's help to accomplish what they have been given to do.

Grab hold of your dream again, hold fast to it, and run with it!

Chapter 15

Finish Your Course With Joy

One thing I do, forgetting those things which are behind and reaching forward to those things which are ahead, I press toward the goal for the prize of the upward call of God in Christ Jesus.

PHILIPPIANS 3:13,14

Are you determined to go all the way in your destiny? Are you ready to say with the apostle Paul, "I've done everything God called me to do. I have been obedient to fulfill the dream He gave me. I have run my race well, and I press on toward the finish line. I am going for the gold. I'm going for the prize of the upward call of God in Christ Jesus."

If you are going to run the race, you have to have strength to get you to the finish line. The Word of God tells us that the joy of the Lord is our strength. (Neh. 8:10.) If you are going to get to the prize of the high calling God has for you, you are going to need the joy of the Lord.

Many Christians have a hard time believing that God actually wants them to enjoy life. They think they have to wear a long face and act like they just swallowed a lemon. They think that if anything is enjoyable, it cannot be from God. If they like it, it must be sin. If it makes them happy, it has to be wrong. In addition, if they see a baby Christian smiling in church, they shake their heads. "What are you doing with that silly grin on your face? Aren't you serious about your salvation? Don't you know how tough it is to be a Christian? What are you doing acting like you are having a good time in church? Don't you know this is the House of Gaaawd?"

As I said before, you have to be careful to whom you listen to. If you're not careful, you'll start to believe that you've got to carry your bottom lip in a wheelbarrow if you're going to make it as a Christian. But that is not what the Word of God says we are to do. There are tons of Scriptures about joy. God is into happiness. Joy was something God came up with. The devil did not come up with it. God did. God wants us to be filled with His joy. He wants us to enjoy what He has given us to do. The devil gets mad when he sees us enjoying our walk with the Lord. He hates it when we have joy, because the joy of the Lord is our strength. If the devil can zap your joy, he is going to get your strength. And if you don't have any strength, it's very hard to run the course God has given you to run.

God is not into weighing us down with all kinds of gloom and depression. He wants us to be able to move freely in all that He has called us to do. If we are weighed down by depression, it is going to slow us down—if we even get up at all.

"Well, yeah," some people say, "but what about Job? Look at everything God did to him. That's not something to be happy about."

God did not beat the snot out of Job! If you will just look at the first and second chapters in the Book of Job, you find that Satan tormented Job. Look at Job 2:7, for instance: "So Satan went out from the presence of the Lord, and struck Job with painful boils from the sole of his foot to the crown of his head." It does not say that God struck Job. It says that Satan struck him. The devil is the one who wants us to suffer. If you will look at the end of the Book of Job, you will see that God not only restored to Job everything that the devil took from him, but God gave him double for his trouble!

"Well," some people argue, "but what about that verse in Psalm 23 where it says, 'Yea, though I walk through the valley of the shadow of death'?" (Ps. 23:4 KJV). Sure, the Bible says that. The problem comes when some people misinterpret what the Bible says. Some people hear this Scripture and think that it says, "You're going to have to suffer all your life in the valley. Then your whole life is going to be one great big valley. That is what it means to be a Christian. If you're going to be a good Christian, you're going to have keep suffering in the valley." That is not what it says. First of all, it says, "though I walk...." It doesn't say, "You've got to walk in the valley." What it is saying is that, even when trials do come, you are going to walk right through the middle of them. Sure, valleys come. But the Bible does not say you have to camp out in them. It does not say you have to stay in the valley of the shadows. No. You get to pass through and walk out on the other side. Psalm 30:5 says, "Weeping may endure for a night, but joy comes in the morning." We are not supposed to build our house in the valley. We are supposed to pass through it.

Isaiah 61:3 says that Jesus came not only to "console those who mourn" but also to "give them beauty for ashes, the oil of joy for mourning, [and] the garment of praise for the spirit of heaviness." Trying to do things without joy is hard. If you are depressed, you get tired and sluggish. Your strength evaporates. How can you fulfill your calling if you are all out of strength?

Jesus told us in John 15:11, "These things I have spoken to you, that My joy may remain in you, and that your joy may be full." Jesus wants us to experience the fullness of joy. He didn't say, "Well, I guess it's okay to smile once in a while, but don't get carried away." No! Jesus said He wants our joy to be full! He wants it to overflow. He wants it to bubble out everywhere we go. He wants it to fill us up and pour out of us like living water.

One time, when I walked into a convenience store for a sandwich, the man behind the counter stepped back and said, "Oh my goodness! You sure look happy today! What are you so excited about?"

"You know what?" I told him. "Jesus has been so good to me."

Well, then he started grinning from ear to ear. "Hey, I know you. I have seen you before. You're that happy preacher."

I like that kind of reputation.

There's Joy in God's Presence

> You will show me the path of life; in Your presence is fullness of joy; at Your right hand are pleasures forevermore.
>
> PSALM 16:11

There is something about just being in God's presence that brings such a pure and beautiful joy. When you are worshiping the Lord with all your heart, soul, might, and strength, there's a refreshing that comes. God longs to hang out with us, to just be with us. So often we get too busy to bask in the presence of God, and we miss all that He has for us.

When is the last time you laid everything aside to just be with Jesus? When is the last time you woke up in the morning with a great big smile on your face and said, "Good morning, Father! I sure do love You." That is enjoying the presence of God. If we'd tap into that, we'd get so filled up that we would start spilling joy everywhere we go.

I know how much I enjoy being with my kids. It blesses me when I know they enjoy my presence, too. There is a little routine my daughter and I love to do together in the morning. We watch this little cartoon on TV, and, when the music kicks in for what they call "The Noodle Dance," Nicole jumps out of my lap and we start doing this fun little dance. "The

Noodle...do the Noodle dance...doom-da-doom-do! Doom-do-doom-do-do-do-do...Do the Noodle!" I spin her around and we dance and have a blast. Then, when the song is over, she jumps back in my lap and we watch the rest of the show together. I know it does not sound very spiritual, but it's fun. We are enjoying each other's company. She enjoys being with me, and I enjoy being with her.

That is what God wants us to be like with Him. If we enjoy being with people we love, how much more should we do that with our heavenly Father? You do not have to get legalistic and super-spiritual about it. You don't have to put on your special prayer voice and get out your kneeling bench. You don't have to wait until you are in church. Just be real with Him. Talk to Him while you are driving down the road in your car.

"Hey, God. I want to say thanks for this great day. I love You, Lord." Lay aside all the religious rigmarole and enjoy the presence of God. God wants us to enjoy His presence in our lives. When we do, it gives us strength and refreshment, because God *is* strength and refreshment. The more we rest in His presence, the more of everything He is will fill us up.

Not only does God want to bless us with the joy of His presence; He wants to bless us with things for our enjoyment. He wants to bless us with health and healing and happy relationships. He wants to bless our finances. If you have kids, you know how much fun it is to buy the things they enjoy. We love to see our kids enjoying the gifts we give them. It thrills our hearts. How much more does our heavenly Father love to give us good things to enjoy?

In 1 Timothy 6:17, we are told to trust in the living God "who gives us richly all things to enjoy." What did that say? You mean the word *enjoy* is in the Bible? Yep. There it is. God gives us things to enjoy. Not only does He want us to enjoy our salvation, our healing, and our deliverance, He wants us to enjoy the houses and cars and clothes and things He gives us.

PURSUING YOUR LIFE DREAM

He wants us to enjoy abundance. Jesus came to give us life more abundantly. (John 10:10.) He wants us to enjoy the tasks He gives us to do. He wants us to enjoy praying, worshiping, and sharing Jesus with the world. He wants us to enjoy life!

God also wants us to enjoy the destiny He has given us. He wants us to enjoy what He has given us to do in life.

I remember getting a telephone call from a good friend of mine who is pastoring a church in Nashville. He and I have done a lot together, and we started pastoring about the same time. So he called me and said, "Eastman, how do you like pastoring?"

I just started laughing. "Man, we're having a blast! Everyone is talking about a summer slump, but we are not having a summer slump here. We are having more visitors than ever. It has been great. People are giving their hearts to the Lord. We are in the middle of revival. Praise God! It's exciting!"

"Did you think it would be this much fun?" he laughed.

"If I had known it was going to be this much fun, I would have done it years ago!"

Many times, when other pastors see me, they will ask me how I like pastoring. "Oh, I love it!" I will say. They look at me like I have eaten too many cocoa puffs or something. "What? You love it?" "Yeah, it's great!" I say. They just look at me as though they think I have lost my mind. Some of these people have pastored for forty years.

I believe God wants us to enjoy what He has called us to do. It should not be drudgery to us. It does not matter if you are called to be an evangelist, a pastor, a plumber, an insurance salesman, or an electrician. God wants you to enjoy yourself. He has paid a very high price for your salvation, so you might as well enjoy the labor that He has given you. I am not saying you do not work hard at it. Of course you do. But it should be so much fun that it doesn't even feel like work.

Sometimes we get letters from people who are upset because I am smiling on TV. Amazing, isn't it? It is true. I guess it must get those religious spirits all stirred up or something. Now, we get tons of wonderful letters too. In fact, for every piece of hate mail we get, we probably get reports from about thirty or forty people who've been born again or baptized in the Holy Spirit while watching our television show or out there at one of our crusades or conventions. I just love getting all the praise reports and testimonies.

However, every so often we will get someone who will say, "How can you be so happy all the time? What's wrong with you? You cannot be that happy. How can you be smiling while people are dying and going to HELL? Aren't you carrying a burden for the world on your shoulders?"

I do not have to carry that kind of weight. Jesus already did that for me. The reason I am smiling is that I am telling people they do not have to die and go to hell. I am telling them good news! If the good news of the gospel is not something to smile about, I do not know what is. I tell you what. That makes me happy! It makes me want to dance and sing and shout! I am telling people about having a relationship with God. I am not feeding them religion. I am not telling them they have to follow a bunch of rules and regulations and wear a long, heavy frown to get in with God. They get to have a relationship with Jesus!

Jesus has blessings for them. He has a happy path for them. He is the One who will give them reason to laugh again. He is the One who is going to bring joy into their hearts. Why shouldn't I be smiling about that?

God Gives Us a Happy Path

Cut through and make firm and plain and smooth, straight paths for your feet [yes, make them safe and upright and happy paths that go in the right direction], so that the lame and halting [limbs] may not be put out of joint, but rather may be cured.

HEBREWS 12:13 AMP

I like how the Amplified version puts it. We have to "cut through" some things to clear a path for our feet. Sometimes we have to cut through the haze and smoke and junk in our lives to get to the happy path God has prepared for us. Sometimes we have to clear away the old religious thinking that is like cobwebs in our way. We have to cut through the wrong thoughts, beliefs, and attitudes to find the joyful destiny God has for us.

Some people think that if they are going to serve God, they are going to have to give up everything they love to do and settle for a life of drudgery. That is so far from the truth. In fact, it's an outright lie from the enemy. Satan doesn't want us to be happy. He wants us to suffer and groan. He wants to kill anything remotely close to joy in our lives. God is into happiness, and He has a happy path for you to take. Happy trails to you! Happy trails to you! Remember the song? I will bet you didn't know that was a godly song. Well, God is the One who has happy trails for you.

Look at verse 13 again. It says we are to make our paths "happy paths that go in the right direction." A happy path takes us in the right direction, and the right direction takes us onto a happy path. Did you get that? What I am trying to say is this: Joy will take you in the right direction God has for you. It will get you there. When you are heading in the direction God has for you, you will be happy. You are going to need the joy of the Lord to get you to your destiny. When you are moving in your destiny, it is going to give you joy.

You are going to have to hold tight to your joy, because the devil would love to steal it from you if you will let him. He would love to rob you of the strength it gives you to run your course and fulfill your dream. However, do not let him do it! Set your face like flint, and be determined not to let any devil, any person, any circumstance, any adversity, or anything steal your joy.

In Chapter 14 we discussed how to hold fast to your dream. You have to do the same thing with your joy. You have to hold on to it with everything in you and refuse to let it go. You are going to need that joy to finish your course. You are going to need it to jump over the hindrances and hurdles along the way. You are going to need it to fulfill the dream God has given you. So hang on to it!

It Takes Joy To Get the Job Done

In Joshua 1:7, God tells Joshua to "be strong and very courageous." That word *strong* in the Hebrew literally means "established, to be firm, to be secure." I see a great fortress in that word. There are times when we have to be like a fortress. We have to take our stand as a child of God and not let the winds of adversity or other people's opinions blow us over. We need to stand strong with a big grin on our face knowing that everything is going to be all right.

Not only did God tell Joshua to be strong, but he also told him to be courageous. If He would have told him only to be courageous, that would have been cool enough, but He tells him to go beyond just courageous. He tells him to be very courageous.

In New Testament Greek, the word for courage is *tharsos*, which is closely related to the Greek word *tharseo*, which is translated "be of good cheer."[1] When you are full of good cheer, you tend to be more courageous. I have noticed this has been true for me. When I am full of joy, I am more daring and bold. Joy helps me stay strong and courageous because the joy of the Lord is my strength. (Neh. 8:10.)

Joy stirs up boldness. When you hang on to your joy, it doesn't matter what other people say or do. You are so intoxicated with the life of God and the joy of Jesus that it does not matter what other people think about you. Have you ever seen anyone get intoxicated with alcohol? Have you ever noticed that if they are really drunk, they do not even care what others think?

The Bible tells us to be filled with the Spirit of God. "Do not be drunk with wine, in which is dissipation; but be filled with the Spirit" (Eph. 5:18). When you are full of the Spirit, you are full of joy, because God is not some long-faced dude who never smiles. God is love, life, and joy. So, go ahead and get drunk on the joy of the Lord. When God calls you to do something and you are filled with the joy of the Lord, it increases your boldness.

When you are tanked up with His presence, intoxicated with His life and His love, it gives you confidence—not a false confidence, but a true confidence to do what God has called you to do. That joy and confidence causes you to be strong and very courageous.

Then God goes on to tell Joshua why he needs to be strong and courageous. "Be strong and very courageous that you may observe to do according to all the law which Moses My servant commanded you; do not turn from it to the right hand or to the left, that you may prosper wherever you go" (Josh. 1:7). He's going to need strength and courage to do all that God has destined him to do. Then the Lord tells him in verse 8, "This Book of the Law shall not depart from your mouth, but you shall meditate in it day and night, that you may observe to do according to all that is written in it."

Why do we meditate on the Word of God? Why do we confess the Word? Why do we memorize and study the Word? Is it like poetry or something nice that just gives you a little peaceful happy thought? Is that why we do it? No. This Book is different than any other book. It is alive. It is active. It is powerful. It is vibrant. It is the very life and power of God. We memorize and confess it so that we will be doers of the Word and not hearers only. (James 1:22.) We are to meditate on the Word of God and not let it depart from our lips so that we may observe to do according to all that is written therein. (Josh. 1:8.) The doer of the Word is blessed.

It is going to take strength and courage to do all that God has called you to do. Where do you get that strength and courage? You guessed it. The joy of the Lord is your strength. There is something about joy that increases our effectiveness. Even in the business world you see it. Those who are the most effective workers are the ones who enjoy what they do, the ones who smile and sing while they work.

Several years ago I was asked to do a conference for *Charisma* magazine in Orlando, Florida. When I got to Orlando, my friend Jake called me up and said he wanted to get together to discuss some ministry things. Well, since I knew there was an electronic expo just down the road from the Charisma conference, I suggested we meet there. I just love gadgets. If you can punch it, pull it, swing it—I am interested. I wanted to check out this electronic expo while I was in town. Jake and I agreed to meet at the registration table. When I got there, I saw Jake with another man beside him. I waved at them, and they both waved back at me. When I went over to them, I shook the other man's hand. "Hi, I'm Eastman Curtis." I just assumed he was with Jake. He introduced himself, then I said, "Hey, Jake. Good to see you."

We went to register for the conference and then walked around to check out all the gadgets. The man I assumed had come along with Jake was very knowledgeable about the electronics, so he was telling me about all this cool stuff. The three of us were laughing and having a great time. Then we decided to grab a bite to eat. So all three of us headed for a restaurant. While we were sitting there eating lunch, he suddenly put his sandwich down and said, "You know something? I am just amazed at you. You are the friendliest people I think I've ever met in my life."

"Well," I said, "that's nice of you to say." At this point, I still thought that Jake knew this man. Jake thought I knew him.

"The thing that really amazes me," he went on, "is that I've had the time of my life hanging around you. You have not talked about getting drunk. You have not talked about women or any of that kind of stuff. You are just talking about God. I am having a great time. I like hanging around you two. You have something going on here."

About that time, Jake and I looked at each other and started to draw the correct conclusion. Now, it may have taken me a while to finally figure out what was going on, but eventually the lights came on. (My wife is usually about ten minutes ahead of me on things like this.) I finally realized that he did not know Jake, but just happened to be there. I cracked up. I told the man, "We just made a friend." Then, after Jake and I hugged on him, I began to tell him about the Lord. In the middle of eating that Reuben sandwich, this man asked Jesus Christ into his heart.

The joy of the Lord drew him. That joy was the magnet that drew him to God. When people see that joy in you, they are drawn to it. They have tried finding it in a bottle. They have tried finding it in a crack pipe or extra-marital affairs or money or cars or boats. When they see the pure joy of the Lord in someone, they know they have not found it in these other things. They see it in you, and they know that is what they want. The joy of the Lord is a magnet.

How To Stir Up the Joy

Sometimes, if you are going through a difficult time, you may need to stir up the joy in you. You need to purpose to hold on to your joy and learn to encourage yourself in the Lord.

1. Praise God

No matter what you are going through, you need to purpose in your heart to keep praising the Lord. Psalm 34:1 says, "I will bless the Lord at all times; His praise shall continually be in my mouth." Purpose to praise the Lord at all times, not just when you feel like it.

2. Encourage Others

When you choose to encourage others, it helps you get your eyes off yourself and your own problems. Proverbs 11:25 NIV says, "He who refreshes others will himself be refreshed." When you need to stir up your joy, find someone to encourage. When you do that, it is going to encourage you. When you reach out to minister to others, it stirs up a fresh joy in your own heart.

3. Hang Around Other Encouragers

As I said in an earlier chapter, it is very important whom you choose to hang out with. If you hang around discouragers, you are going to be pulled down. You have to find encouragers to build you up. Find people who talk about the things of God with passion. Find positive people. Find other people filled with the joy of the Lord. Find people who are visionaries. Hang around them. Let their joy rub off on you.

Run With Joy

Joy is the fuel for strength to run. Joy is what you need to keep tanked up on in order to move in your destiny and finish the race set before you. The fuel will get you to the finish line. Without it, you are going to run out of gas before you get to the first freeway. If you are going to finish your course, don't ever turn loose of your joy.

Jesus said, "My yoke is easy and My burden is light" (Matt. 11:30). Have you ever tried to run while carrying something heavy? It's not easy, is it? Jesus said His yoke is easy and His burden is light. It's not hard. It is not some heavy, cumbersome old cross you have to lug around all your life. Religious people will try to strap all kinds of heavy things on you and tell you that you have to do this, that, and the other to keep your salvation. That is not what Jesus said. It would be hard to run with the vision (Hab. 2:2), if it were too heavy for us to carry. God is not into loading us up with all kinds of heavy weights. He wants us to be free to run the race set before us without a heavy, religious yoke holding us down.

So, fling off the things that weigh you down and go for the prize of the high calling of God. Run for the gold! And finish your course with joy!

Endnotes

Chapter 3

[1] www.kodak.com, "George Eastman."

[2] www.pbs.org, "Henry Ford."

Chapter 5

[1] *Webster's New World College Dictionary,* "stronghold," p. 1329.

[2] Thayer, "profiting," #4298.

Chapter 11

[1] Strong's, "offence," # 4625.

Chapter 15

[1] Strongs, "tharseo," #2293.

References

The New Strong's Exhaustive Concordance of the Bible. Thomas Nelson Publishers. Nashville, TN 1990.

Thayer and Smith. "Greek Lexicon entry for Prokopto." "The KJV New Testament Greek Lexicon." <http://www.biblestudytools.net/Lexicons/Greek/grk.cgi?number=4298&version=kjv>.

Webster's New World College Dictionary, Third Edition. Simon and Schuster, Inc. New York, NY 1997.

www.kodak.com, History of Kodak, Eastman Kodak Company, 1994-2001.

www.pbs.org, On the Line, PBS 1995-2001.

Prayer of Salvation

God loves you—no matter who you are, no matter what your past. God loves you so much that He gave His one and only begotten Son for you. The Bible tells us that "...whoever believes in him shall not perish but have eternal life" (John 3:16 NIV). Jesus laid down His life and rose again so that we could spend eternity with Him in heaven and experience His absolute best on earth. If you would like to receive Jesus into your life, say the following prayer out loud and mean it from your heart.

Heavenly Father, I come to You admitting that I am a sinner. Right now, I choose to turn away from sin, and I ask You to cleanse me of all unrighteousness. I believe that Your Son, Jesus, died on the cross to take away my sins. I also believe that He rose again from the dead so that I might be forgiven of my sins and made righteous through faith in Him. I call upon the name of Jesus Christ to be the Savior and Lord of my life. Jesus, I choose to follow You and ask that You fill me with the power of the Holy Spirit. I declare that right now I am a child of God. I am free from sin and full of the righteousness of God. I am saved in Jesus' name. Amen.

If you prayed this prayer to receive Jesus Christ as your Savior for the first time, please contact us on the Web at **www.harrisonhouse.com** to receive a free book.

Or you may write to us at:
Harrison House
P.O. Box 35035
Tulsa, Oklahoma 74153

About the Author

Eastman Curtis is an internationally known speaker, author, and television minister. He has reached hundreds of thousands through his internationally aired television show "This Generation," thirty-minute specials on many Fox affiliates, appearances on "The 700 Club" as a guest host, and a 60-second salvation commercial on MTV. Eastman has also produced several volumes of 90-second radio devotionals which have been enjoyed by audiences nationwide on over 500 stations for their practical and humorous teaching on real life issues.

Eastman travels the world preaching in churches, conferences, and ministry seminars, where he challenges teenagers and adults to fulfill God's destiny for their lives. He also hosts powerful, life-changing weekend crusades for young adults known as "This Generation Convention."

Eastman Curtis Ministries is located in Broken Arrow, Oklahoma, where they started Destiny Church. This has fulfilled a dream that has been in their hearts for many years. Eastman and Angel live in Tulsa, Oklahoma, where they are raising their son and daughter, Sumner and Nicole.

To contact Eastman Curtis,
please write to:

Eastman Curtis Ministries
P.O. Box 470290
Tulsa, OK 74147

*Please include your prayer requests
and comments when you write.*

Other Books by Eastman Curtis

Xtreme Talk for Teens

Additional copies of this book
are available from your local bookstore.

HARRISON HOUSE
Tulsa, Oklahoma 74153

www.harrisonhouse.com

Fast. Easy. Convenient!

- ◆ New Book Information
- ◆ Look Inside the Book
- ◆ Press Releases
- ◆ Bestsellers

- ◆ Free E-News
- ◆ Author Biographies
- ◆ Upcoming Books
- ◆ Share Your Testimony

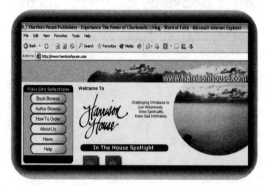

For the latest in book news and author information, please visit us on the Web at www.harrisonhouse.com. Get up-to-date pictures and details on all our powerful and life-changing products. Sign up for our e-mail newsletter, *Friends of the House,* and receive free monthly information on our authors and products including testimonials, author announcements, and more!

Harrison House—
Books That Bring Hope, Books That Bring Change

The Harrison House Vision

Proclaiming the truth and the power

Of the Gospel of Jesus Christ

With excellence;

Challenging Christians to

Live victoriously,

Grow spiritually,

Know God intimately.